D1345436

TO THE LINKSLAND

ALSO BY THE AUTHOR

The Green Road Home

TO THE LINKSLAND

A GOLFING ADVENTURE

MICHAEL
BAMBERGER

VIKING

VIKING
Published by the Penguin Group
Viking Penguin, a division of Penguin Books USA Inc.,
375 Hudson Street, New York, New York 10014, U.S.A.
Penguin Books Ltd, 27 Wrights Lane, London W8 5TZ, England
Penguin Books Australia Ltd, Ringwood, Victoria, Australia
Penguin Books Canada Ltd, 10 Alcorn Avenue, Suite 300, Toronto, Ontario, Canada M4V 3B2
Penguin Books (N.Z.) Ltd, 182–190 Wairau Road, Auckland 10, New Zealand

Penguin Books Ltd, Registered Offices:
Harmondsworth, Middlesex, England

First published in 1992 by Viking Penguin,
a division of Penguin Books USA Inc.

1 3 5 7 9 10 8 6 4 2

Copyright © Michael Bamberger, 1992
All rights reserved

LIBRARY OF CONGRESS CATALOGING-IN-PUBLICATION DATA
Bamberger, Michael, 1960–
To the linksland : a golfing adventure / Michael Bamberger.
p. cm.
ISBN 0-670-84182-X
1. Bamberger, Michael, 1960– . 2. Caddies—United States—
Biography. 3. Sportswriters—United States—Biography. 4. Golf—
Scotland. I. Title.
GV964.B36A3 1992
796.352'092—dc20
[B] 92-7902

Printed in the United States of America
Set in Garamond No. 3
Designed by Brian Mulligan

Without limiting the rights under copyright
reserved above, no part of this publication
may be reproduced, stored in or introduced into
a retrieval system, or transmitted, in any form
or by any means (electronic, mechanical, photo-
copying, recording or otherwise), without the
prior written permission of both the copyright
owner and the above publisher of this book.

For my
adventuresome wife,
with love

CARD OF THE COURSE

PART TWO: *Coming In*

PART ONE

GOING OUT

You may take it from me that there are two kinds of golf;
there is golf—and tournament golf. And they
are not at all the same thing.

—Robert T. Jones, Jr.
DOWN THE FAIRWAY

CHAPTER ONE

Out

I THINK THE MAN LIKED MY WIFE. He kept saying to her, "If you want to eat, eat now. No food till we get to Port Bou." He was a trim man, with long white sideburns and a tiny head, and his clothes—his sneakers and pants and vest and cap—all bore the crest of a great sporting-goods manufacturer. His voice, warm and slightly drunk, sounded vaguely familiar. I had never before met this little man, and yet I felt I knew him. Who was he? Where had I heard that burr? He looked at my golf bag. I looked at his crests. He looked at my wife. No introduction seemed necessary.

Why were we there, newlyweds, sitting on the cold floor of a train station in St. Raphael, a small seaside cathedral town in the south of France? Because the wooden benches were filled with sleeping soldiers returning from war. Because we had nowhere else to be—we had given up our apartments, our jobs, our former lives. Because, just like the little man standing before us, we were waiting for the overnight train to Port Bou, working our way to the next stop, and trying to beat a night's rent doing it.

I wondered if he would be in our compartment. A private cabin was not in our budget. A month earlier, we had been rich:

I had been a reporter on *The Philadelphia Inquirer* and my wife had managed big accounts for a New York advertising agency. We had ridden in taxicabs. But in February of 1991 she quit her job and I took a leave from mine so that I could become a caddie on the European golf tour and so that she could join me. I did not have to convince her. The tour stopped in Paris and Madrid, London and Florence, Brussels and Milan, the Scottish highlands, the north coast of Portugal, the south of France. We wanted adventure. We wanted to be *overseas.* The very word excited us. We wanted to open our lives to surprise. Some people said we were dropping out. One person asked if my move, from reporter to caddie, was "lateral." The answer, I suppose, depends on how you view newspapering and how you view caddying and if you know what it means to make a lateral move. I wanted to lead the life of the professional amateur, the man who earns a living wage, and not more, for being around the thing that consumes him, the thing that fascinates him, the thing that he loves. My wife wanted to travel.

Maybe I sound like the guy who corners you in the cafeteria at lunch on Monday and relives for your benefit every stroke he took in his Sunday game. I am not that guy. With rare exception, I am not interested in the rounds of golf I've played. My best games are ahead of me. I fully believe that, now. It is the promise of improvement that makes golf captivating. We all want to improve, but how do we know if we have? Normally, in this world, we must rely on the evaluations of others. But in golf, in so many ways a bodiless game, the results are wholly tangible. *How many whacks?* Each player must decide for himself if he is improving. Golf can be selfish, which is its weakness, but it requires honesty, which is its ultimate strength. I didn't know this stuff a year ago, before my travels. But the trip changed my thinking, it changed me. I am seemingly the same person on the outside but strangely altered internally.

As my wife and I were packing in February of 1991, deciding what to bring and what to leave behind, I was afraid to tell my friends, family, colleagues, and bosses the truest purpose, the ultimate goal, of my trip. I feared that it sounded so small. Now

I realize the true size of its scope, and I'd like to tell you because I think you'll understand and because I am no longer afraid: I wanted to improve.

I remember the day when I first realized I needed help. I was on the practice tee of a Palm Beach resort, lashing at striped balls with a sort of desperate energy. Next to me was an old hunched man, a man of wealth and accomplishment long done pushing ninety, slapping one meek ground ball after another in the general direction of a fifty-yard marker. A youth working the range, a collegian of mindless good cheer, watched a single swing and announced, "You're hitting them well today, Mr. Hartmann." And Mr. Hartmann turned slowly on his spikes, leaned on his driver, and said, "Young sir, I am running out of time." And right then I came to a realization: *I am Mr. Hartmann; I am that man!*

But why did I have to become a caddie on the European golf tour in order to seek betterment? Why couldn't I just go to one of those golf schools in Arizona or Florida or New Mexico? Because the golf schools are held on courses financed by the sale of condominiums. Because they are run by men trying to make money. Because the instructors are experts in a narrow area, the golf *swing.* I wanted to make a study of the game.

I wanted to search for the primal heart of golf, which has been subverted in the United States by hundred-dollar green fees and five-hour rounds and motorized carts and private-club snobbishness and numbing golf telecasts in which touring professionals, the players who embody our notion of golfing excellence, toil laboriously. The European tour struck me as a vast and unexplored territory. In the back pages of *Golf World* there always seemed to be a picture of a ruddy-faced professional wiping windblown hair out of his eyes with one hand as he reached for a driver with the other, and the cutline had something about so-and-so's play in the French Open or the Portuguese Open or the Spanish Open or the Irish Open. The European tour seemed exciting, loose, and fun. I knew it was producing players unlike anything we had in the United States: Ian Woosnam, a tiny Welshman of unbridled strength and a fiery temper; Bernhard Langer, a stoical German with manic dedication to precision; Sandy Lyle, a large, amiable Scotsman who played large, amiable golf; José-María Olazábal, a Spaniard engrossed in a quest for mastery and uninterested in swing mechanics; Nick Faldo, an Englishman obsessed with swing mechanics in his quest for mastery; and Severiano Ballesteros, the Spanish *artista,* the most captivating golfer in the world. The Europeans, with Ballesteros as their prototype, were players of creativity and flair and style.

That's what American golfers used to be. For most of the twentieth century, the best U. S. golfers were indisputably the kings of all golfdom: first Jones, then Hogan, briefly Palmer, then Nicklaus, and lastly Watson. Everybody studied them. But something insidious happened to American golfers after Watson's reign. They became stagnant. I did not think the players I saw on TV and at American tournaments could truly be the high priests of world golf. If they were, they would have shown more vitality, more vigor—there would have been an aura enveloping them. In the 1950s, players used to weasel their way into practice games with Hogan because they wanted to rub up against his magic. Who had the magic now? Where could I find it? At the Shearson Lehman Hutton Open? I didn't think so. At the Scottish Open? A definite possibility.

Scotland itself was a dream. I viewed it as a homeland: the place where the game took root centuries ago, but also, I hoped, the place where the game breathed free. In the United States, golf and class-consciousness were inextricably (and needlessly) bound. I imagined golf in Scotland as a true national pastime, an activity that linked a citizenry that *liked* the idea of finding common ground. In my mind, Scotland was a place where the crunching sound of cleats against the brick floor of a clubhouse served as an invitation to play nine more, starting in the long, late dusk and holing final putts by the light of the moon. Scotland, I figured, would be good for my game. It was in need of help. I was mired in a thirteen-year slump. That is to say, from the time I first became infatuated with the game, as an eighth-grader taking golf in gym class, through the summer of '78, after my senior year of high school, I steadily improved. And then I began a long period of deterioration. I was never your prototypical duffer. My game had the superficial veneer of competence. But something wasn't clicking. The head-to-body messages were coming in garbled. I could not stop flailing away at the ball. I think I lacked inner peace. Or maybe I just stank.

All through the decline, my love for the game was unwavering—intensifying, actually. I don't think I was like the man who grows increasingly obsessed with the woman he cannot have (although I don't discount that possibility, either). My unsatisfying play opened new vistas. I found that the more interested I became in golf, the more interesting the game became.

That happens. In time, the physicist in you becomes fascinated by swing mechanics. The psychologist in you becomes interested in the mind's control over the body; the architect in course design; the engineer in club design; the sociologist in the interaction of golfers; the mathematician in gambling odds; the accountant in score-keeping; the lawyer in rules; the historian in the golf of preceding generations.

And the dreamer in you becomes fascinated by professional golf. Golf is strange that way. Almost every person who plays follows professional golf with something approaching befuddlement. More than any other athlete, the professional golfer looks normal; his physical ordinariness is a ubiquitous reminder of our limitations. *So what makes him so special?* That's one of the reasons I became a caddie on the U. S. golf tour in 1985—I wanted to get closer to the people who seemed closer to figuring the game out. I wanted to be immersed in the world of golf, surrounded by all the tilted theories it generates and helpless devotees it attracts. When I got out there, I discovered that the pros were a lot like us; they were worried about hooked drives and pushed iron shots and stubbed putts, just like you and me. The chief difference was their standards. I remember caddying for a tour player who became enraged after fouling up a simple shot. He had intended to draw a 7-iron shot and keep the ball below the hole but instead the shot faded and finished twenty feet above the hole. He turned red and purple and declared publicly his worthlessness. He grabbed the putter from me and funneled all his temporary hatred for the game into effort and sank that twenty-footer. Do you think he smiled after the birdie? He did not. Oh, I loved being out there.

The summer of 1990 was too hectic. I was covering the Philadelphia Phillies for my paper, *The Philadelphia Inquirer.* I proposed to Christine in June, in Chicago, a few hours before a Cubs-Phillies matinee. Christine was living and working in New York but was often on the road. I was often on the road. Our roads crossed too infrequently. A few days after the final game of the 1990 World Series we were married. A few days after that we were in Haiti, on our honeymoon, and I was fast discovering what it meant to be married to an adventurer. It was the first of November, the day after Halloween and a voodoo holy day. The air smelled of spices and there were hissing sounds from the bushes. Haiti had been her idea.

"Well, what do you think we should do?" I asked.

"Find a voodoo ceremony," she said. In the past year, she had been in the Amazonian jungle and on safari in Africa.

"I meant in our married lives."

"Keep exploring," she said.

Three months later, she quit her job and I took a one-year leave from mine. We sublet our New York apartment and gave up the one in Philadelphia. We packed up two suitcases, I put a golf bag over my shoulder, and on the twenty-fourth of February we headed off for St. Raphael and the Mediterranean Open, the first big stop on the European golf tour's 1991 season. Our plan was loose: I'd caddie our way to Scotland, and then we'd go exploring. I made wallet-sized copies of the tour schedule (through the Scottish Open) for both of us.

DATES	TOURNAMENT	LOCATION
Feb. 28–March 3	Mediterranean Open	St. Raphael, France
March 7–10	Balearic Islands Open	Majorca, Spain

March 14–17	Catalonia Open	Tarragona, Spain
March 21–24	Portuguese Open	Oporto, Portugal
March 28–31	Florence Open	Florence, Italy
April 11–14	Jersey Open	Jersey, United Kingdom
April 18–21	Benson & Hedges International	St. Mellion, England
April 25–28	Madrid Open	Madrid, Spain
May 2–5	Cannes Open	Cannes, France
May 9–12	Spanish Open	Madrid, Spain
May 16–19	Italian Open	Milan, Italy
May 24–27	P. G. A. Championship	Virginia Water, England
May 30–June 2	British Masters	Woburn, England
June 6–9	Murphy's Cup	York, England
June 13–16	Belgian Open	Waterloo, Belgium
June 20–23	Irish Open	Killarney, Ireland
June 27–30	French Open	Paris, France
July 3–6	Monte Carlo Open	Monte Carlo, Monaco
July 10–13	Scottish Open	Auchterarder, Scotland

One morning, early in that first week on the Côte d'Azur, I left our little hotel, shabby but adequate, shortly after six, seeking coffee and a croissant and a ride to the course. The fog was lifting off the streets of St. Raphael and daylight was breaking. Across the street and out of the glimmer a body emerged, little and trim and wearing a cap. I couldn't tell if the body belonged to a player or an official or a caddie, but it definitely belonged to golf. He called out to me, with a hint of a brogue, "All right?" It was a welcoming.

Now, as I write down this little memoir of my golfing adventure, I remember. Now I know why the voice at the train station—the one advising us to eat then or wait for Port Bou—sounded familiar. The voice belonged to the man who had welcomed me back to golf.

CHAPTER TWO

TERAVAINEN

FOR A LONG TIME, in the agate type of newspaper columns, I had followed the distinctive Finnish name of Peter Teravainen. I knew from golfing friends that he had been born and raised in Massachusetts and educated at Yale, and that he was living in Singapore and studying Buddhism with his Singaporean Buddhist wife. Teravainen was described as a hard-swinging, theory-spewing touring professional in his mid-thirties, the son of a gym teacher and a nurse, who reveled in the rough-hewn golfing life he had made for himself playing the European tour. I had written to Peter before our departure, asking him for a job as his caddie. I cited my previous work experience. He wrote back and said he'd take me on for two tournaments. After that, I'd be on my own.

I met him for the first time two days before the start of the Mediterranean Open in St. Raphael. Peter turned out to be a heartily built bespectacled man of nearly six feet, with thinning brownish-blond hair, strong tanned hands, and a lined, intelligent face anchored by a sturdy nose. He had small teeth, a broad forehead, pale blue eyes, and perfectly manicured fingernails, which somehow prevented him from looking haggard.

"I play a full schedule," Teravainen said on our first day

together. We were climbing up and down the hills of a contrived Robert Trent Jones development course—the venue for the Mediterranean Open—and I had his bag on my back. I was a caddie again, and I was happy. "I feel that if there's a golf tournament somewhere and they're offering money and I can get in, I should be there." In the previous week, Peter had played in a small tournament in Girona, Spain, and after it he made the two-day drive to St. Raphael in a two-door rental car, sharing the cramped space with his traveling partner, Bill Malley, a former U. S. Public Links champion; Bill's wife, Rose; two huge golf bags; and half a dozen suitcases. Prior to Girona, Peter had planned to play in a tournament in Dubai, United Arab Emirates, but it had been canceled—Peter thought unnecessarily—because of the war in the Gulf. So he played instead in a tournament in Singapore, his adopted homeland.

He was starting his tenth year on the European tour. He first came over in 1982 because he couldn't earn a spot on the lucrative U. S. tour. Though there was far less money on the European tour, there was far less competition, too. Before long, he was a regular.

In 1984, Peter played twenty-three tournaments in twenty-three weeks, with the burden of rugged travel between stops—ferries, rental cars, trains, buses, stand-by flights—always with the bag on his back and a suitcase in each hand. He thought nothing of playing in ten or eleven consecutive events. In Europe, most players regard five or six straight weeks as beyond grueling and on the U. S. tour four or five is considered the outer limit. Even three successive tournaments can turn a player's brain to mush: in a professional stroke-play competition, money changes hands on every shot and the stress can be overwhelming. To play as much as he wanted to play, Peter had to find ways to reduce the stress. That's why several years ago he stopped gambling during practice rounds. Some players want something at stake during their practice games so they can simulate the emotions of tournament play. Others need to make money; on the European tour there are still players trying to pay their motel rents through extracurricular play, as there once were on the U. S.

tour. Peter's retirement from gambling put him in the minority. But he figured his mind was burdened enough during the four competitive rounds that comprise the typical tour event (two qualifying rounds, followed by a thirty-six-hole cut that eliminates about half the field, and then two more rounds). He viewed practice rounds as a chance to commune with the course. Often he played by himself, first thing in the morning, without even a warm-up. Before long, I realized that some of Peter's colleagues thought of him as antisocial, but that was a misunderstanding. He was just trying to preserve himself.

A friend once suggested to Peter that he might play better, and make more money, by competing in fewer events, but Peter ignored the suggestion, even though he acknowledged that it might be true. He believed that the life of a touring professional must include struggle: play hard, sleep rough, travel cheap, carry cash.

Teravainen developed certain attitudes toward his profession early in his career and they have stuck. In 1980 and 1981, he attempted to play the U. S. tour, but his game was too undeveloped and he found himself always scraping to get to the next stop. He thought of his hardscrabble existence as a sort of apprenticeship until the day he realized it was, in fact, a way of life. That day came in the winter of 1980, during a practice round for a Monday qualifying round for the Bay Hill Classic, a tour event in Orlando, Florida. Peter and two other young players had joined up with Mike Hill, a thickly calloused veteran. They were sitting on a bench, waiting for the group in front of them to get out of range when the discussion turned to John Cook.

"Who in the hell is John Cook?" Hill said.

Teravainen was surprised; he figured everybody knew who John Cook was.

"He's a former U. S. Amateur champ," somebody piped up cheerfully. Cook won the title in 1978, the year Teravainen graduated from Yale.

Hill thought the comment came from Peter and stared at him. "Amateur golf," he said, "don't mean shit."

Peter was embarrassed, but he immediately understood Hill's

meaning: amateur golf was a pleasant diversion; professional golf was a life, a life of struggle that allowed no time for niceties like amateurism. For Teravainen, that one terse comment from Hill proved to be important in his professional education. It helped him develop his credo.

Since turning professional in 1979, Peter has had one goal above all others: to make a living solely by playing tournament golf, and to make it without the accoutrements common to the modern pro. As much as he can, he tries to go it alone. When I met Peter, he had no teaching guru, no travel agent, no manager, no psychologist, no equipment endorsements, no professional caddie, no clothing contract. He wanted to stay independent. He felt corrupting influences lurked everywhere.

I did not see him in danger of being offered a clothing deal. For any clothing manufacturer, an association with Peter would be dangerous. There was nobody left on the European tour, and probably nobody left in golf, who dressed like Peter. He was a fashion renegade.

Starting in the 1960s, and right through the middle of the 1980s, there was a uniform for the professional golfer adopted worldwide: snug polyester pants with built-in belts, often plaid but sometimes brown, worn with Munsingwear shirts, usually white or yellow, with stiff pointed collars.

Then there was a revolution. Golfers, lagging several years behind the rest of the free world, discovered the so-called preppie look: loose cotton pants, often khaki-colored, with four pockets and without a built-in belt, worn with loose-fitting polo shirts with soft, rounded collars. (Since then, there has been a counterwave, a drift toward loudness affecting only those players who will wear anything if they are paid enough money: shirts patterned with large, bright, dizzying geometric shapes, lavender sweaters with two-foot-high nineteenth-century golfers embroidered on the fronts.)

Peter took no part in the revolution. Had his sartorial tastes been influenced by the stereotypical dress codes of his schools —before Yale, he had attended the Tabor Academy, a prep school in Marion, Massachusetts—you might have expected him to feel right at home in the khakis and polos. If he had been modestly rebellious, you might have expected him to go one step further, to preppie dishabille: wear the khakis rumpled, wear the polo shirts faded, maybe wear red socks. But Peter, who attended both Tabor and Yale on scholarship, was a reactionary: he borrowed his style straight from Mike Hill, circa 1970, and held on to it. The collars on Peter's golf shirts were stiff enough to accommodate a tie. His favorite pants, made of wholly unnatural fibers, were slate gray and shiny, with an off-white pinstriping, tight at the hips and thighs, then slightly flaring from the knee to the tops of his shoes. Great trousers. He wore them twice in that first week on the Côte d'Azur.

His swing was distinctive, too. Teravainen belonged to the brute force school; off the tee, he was as long as anybody. Occasionally during his swing he grunted. Teravainen had so much unspent energy at the traditional concluding point for a full swing—hands neck-high, with the shaft of the club over the shoulder and pointing down the back—that he sometimes swung the club again, hard and in reverse, returning to his starting point. Among his colleagues, Peter's swing had a nickname: the Whiplash. Once, in a tournament in Switzerland, Peter swung so hard he fainted and in the fall sprained an arm. Peter's swing was unteachable. It came from within.

People said that if he refined his swing, there was no telling what he might do. But Peter was not interested. He expected that the refining period would cost him money—professional golfers are usually flubs when they are making changes—and by the time the adjustments took effect, *if* they took effect, Peter feared he would be too old for tournament golf. Moreover, seeking refinement would have required Peter to have a teacher, and that was not something he wanted.

That's unusual. Virtually every player on the U. S. tour has a person to whom they entrust their swing. Most players on the European tour, although a smaller percentage than on the U. S. tour, have golfing mentors, too. There are tournament weeks in which Faldo has his teacher, David Leadbetter, follow him around for eight or more hours a day: four on the course, a couple on the practice tee, a couple on the putting green. Bob Torrance—the father of Sam Torrance, a perennial Ryder Cup player—was formerly a Scottish club professional who now travels the European tour full time, giving instruction to a score of players, including Woosnam. Sandy Lyle, a former Masters and British Open champion, returns to his father, a retired club professional. There are notable exceptions. Ballesteros is largely self-taught and has no regular coach, although he'll talk to just about anybody. Olazábal is completely self-tutored. If he has a problem, he works it out himself. Teravainen's just the same.

Peter has his own method. His hands are low at address. In his grip, Peter's left thumb is exposed, in contrast to classical instruction, which preaches that the left thumb must be covered by the right hand. In his take-away, Teravainen defies the modern method, for he does not fan the club face open. Instead, he brings the clubhead back in a shut position, with the toe of the club pointing to *terra firma,* a somewhat Palmeresque move. Peter has a massive hip turn and shoulder turn and at impact, and in a blur, he throws his hands through the ball with a mighty, last-second flick. *Boom!* His swing is not lovely or pretty or poetic. It's deadly.

From the time he took up the game at age nine, through his graduation from Yale, Peter, for the most part, taught himself. He was the Ivy League golf champion in his junior and senior years and he was one of the better amateur golfers in New England in the late 1970s. But his game was not nearly advanced enough to earn him a living as a touring pro, which is what he wanted to be. So, after college he sought professional counsel for the first time. Peter drove to Florida in a borrowed van and took a job as a cocktail waiter at a rambling old golf resort called the Belleview Biltmore in Clearwater. When the Yale men on their annual winter trip to the hotel discovered that the person fetching their drinks was a fellow Blue attempting professional golf, they'd chuckle and ask, "Seriously, what is it that you intend to do with your life?" Teravainen didn't stick around to answer. He was playing golf every morning with a bartender and a piano player, hitting balls every afternoon and taking lessons thrice-weekly from a man named Irv Schloss. The first time Schloss looked at Peter's unorthodox, closed backswing he said, "You've got the best backswing of any player I've ever seen. Never let anybody talk you out of it." That was the major thought Peter took from Schloss, who died in 1984. Peter has not had a teacher since.

Unlike most professionals, Peter never sought an equipment contract, even after his best year, the year of Schloss's death, when he finished fifteenth on the European tour's Order of Merit. (The Order of Merit is the European tour's gently worded equivalent of the U. S. tour's "money list." Peter's fifteenth-place finish in 1984 earned him £40,503, equal then to about $55,000; Jack Nicklaus finished fifteenth on the U. S. money list that same year and won $272,595.) Teravainen plays Ping clubs, and has since 1981, because he likes them, because they're free, and because they come without compromising encumbrances.

Ping writes checks at the conclusion of the season to the players who use their clubs; the size of the check is based solely on how much the player earns in tournament play. The percentage rises as a player earns more—top players can double their income with the year-end bonus, while middle-of-the-pack players might increase their earnings by ten percent with the post-season Ping check. But the company has no star system, no special contracts for big names. Every player begins the season under identical terms. The Ping player is not obligated to appear in any advertising or play in any corporate outings or appear at any social functions. Peter liked that. The Ping player is required to do only two things: employ at least nine Ping clubs, out of the fourteen clubs to which the rules limit a player, and carry the clubs in a Ping golf bag, an unaesthetic white, plastic sack with the company name pasted on the sides, lettered in a type style one might call computer text. Peter didn't find his standards jeopardized by any of that.

Peter didn't often need the cumbersome Ping bag, so the company gave him a small collapsible carry bag, the same model used by weekend golfers. He employed it when he caddied for himself, or when his wife, Veronica, caddied for him. He seldom employed one of the hundred or so roaming caddies who travel the tour; the few that he liked were out of his budget. And Veronica, living with her mother in Singapore and working as a United Airlines flight attendant, wasn't often around. Sometimes Peter hired a local teenager to carry his bag, but often, especially on the Continent, where the game is still taking root, local caddies weren't available. In those instances, Peter didn't mind carrying his own bag, which the European tour rules allow. (On the U. S. tour, each player is required to have his own caddie.) He figured he played just as well without a caddie as with one. As he explained this to me, I had the feeling that his approach to the use of caddies was just like all his other golfing decisions, ultimately rooted in his desire to keep costs down, to make it on his own, to have total independence, to succeed by himself, and to share blame for his failures with nobody.

I left my former life behind the moment I threw the strap of Peter's big Ping bag over my left shoulder. At *The Philadelphia Inquirer* I was in The Newspaper Guild and every week I received a paycheck. On the European tour, I was at Peter's mercy. With the British economy in a tailspin, there were scores of men, and a few women, traveling the tour, seeking caddie jobs. Certainly, there were more caddies than jobs. The handwriting was plain: if I could not earn a full-time job with Peter, I'd have trouble. And without steady caddie work, the whole concept of the trip was endangered.

Peter told me that he was an easy loop, but that was only his opinion. I fast realized that he was superstitious, fastidious, and finicky. And I fast realized that whatever caddie skills I had developed on the U. S. tour in 1985 had been pushed to the farthest recesses of my brain. I had to get back my caddie legs in a hurry, and to reacquaint myself with the caddie mentality.

Early on, Peter told me that the clubs were rattling too much when I walked. I wanted to say, "Peter, don't you realize that the rhythmic clanking of clubheads is one of the great sounds produced by the game?" Instead I wrapped the towel around the clubs in a serpentine pattern, held a hand around the towel, and kept the clubs, and myself, quiet.

At the start of our first round together Peter handed me three new balls—balata-covered, 100-compression Titleist 384s, each stamped with the numeral 8—and I was expected to give him the balls, as he needed them, in the particular order in which he wanted them. I found it difficult to distinguish one ball from the other, but Peter did not: he had custom-marked each ball with a series of elaborate pencil dots—the balls had no inherent order, but he had assigned them one. I think it was his attempt to reduce the innate capriciousness of the game.

Yet at other times, he succumbed to the game's mysticism. Peter played with balls stamped with an 8 because the numeral eight, he learned from his wife, was an ancient Chinese symbol for prosperity. Veronica also taught him the dangerous potency of red: Peter felt that wearing red set him up for an extraordinary round, one way or the other. Clothes, in general, were powerful to him: if he started a round in the cool of early morning in a heavy wool sweater and played well, the sweater stayed on, no matter how hot the day grew, until he made a bogey. He was particular about eating, too. If a specific breakfast served as a prelude to a 69 on a Thursday, which is what he shot in our first round together, he'd have the identical breakfast on Friday. "When you're going good," he said, "you don't change a thing." When Peter was on a cut-making roll, he didn't change drivers, putters, or even headcovers. I wondered if he extended that policy to caddies.

That Thursday opening round at St. Raphael went well. The weather was sunny and pleasant and Peter was relaxed and hitting the straight ball. On that day, he *was* an easy loop. Easy day, easy loop. But the Friday round, during which a steady rain fell unceasingly, was a different matter.

The ground was so wet that every time the ball landed it became encrusted with mud. A golf ball is difficult enough to hit without a half-ounce of glob sticking to its side, so the tournament officials invoked a rule allowing players to lift, clean, and place their ball when it was on the fairway. On one hole, Peter marked the position of his ball, picked it up, and tossed it to me for a cleaning. While I wiped the dirt off and returned the ball to white, he walked ahead a hundred yards or so, umbrella in hand, to survey his ensuing shot. I put the ball in my pocket, to keep it warm, safe, and dry. Eventually, Peter returned with his palm stuck out—he wanted his ball back. I remember thinking, *He's waiting; he's waiting; don't keep him waiting.* I shoved a hand into a pocket and pulled out a ball and placed it on his outstretched palm. He returned the ball to the marked spot on the fairway and pulled a club from the bag.

Suddenly a realization came over me and I felt sick. In my haste I had shoved the wrong hand into the wrong pocket and pulled out the wrong ball! A player can't change a ball during a hole unless the ball is damaged, and only then with the approval of his playing partners. If Peter played the wrong ball, he'd be cheating! I alerted Peter to my mistake.

Peter examined the pencil dots on the wrong ball while I produced the correct one. He was kind. All he said was, "Never put the ball in your pocket." He sounded like a Kennedy: *Neva put the ball in yaw pocket.* That was it.

I didn't think I could do much worse; I had nearly caused him a two-shot penalty, and probably incalculable psychic harm. But a few holes later I goofed again, and worse.

Peter routinely drank four or five cups of coffee before a round and he flew around the course. To keep up with him between shots I practically had to run. The worse he played, the faster he walked. And he was not playing well in that second round.

On the tenth hole, he drove his ball under a tree. At first, he considered punching out with a 7-iron. He gave the club a few waggles and decided he'd be better off with an eight, so he handed the seven back to me. He played his shot (hitting the ball fat, striking about a half-inch of earth first) and set off after it. I replaced the divot and went chasing after him. Eventually, he finished the hole and we moved on.

As we gathered on the eleventh tee, I saw a man wearing knee-high rubber boots and waxed jacket, yelling in French, waving a golf club, and walking fast in our direction. Peter said to his two playing partners, "Anybody lose a club?" He said to me, "You lose a club?"

I was just starting to say, "I don't think so," when I dipped my head into the bag and saw, to my horror, that there were only thirteen clubs in it. When I looked up the Frenchman was on the tee, standing in front of me, holding Peter's 7-iron and smiling idiotically. One of the other caddies snickered. I felt myself turning red. I knew that within a day virtually everybody on the European tour would know that I had lost a 7-iron.

Did you hear what that guy working for Teravainen did?

Which guy, that ganky-looking American?

Yeah—he lost Tera's 7-iron!

You kidding me?

No, he lost the bloody thing—hasn't been seen since.

Caddies would tell players. Players would tell wives. Wives would tell other wives. Those wives would tell their husbands. Those husbands would tell their caddies. Before long, the 7-iron would turn into a putter, and the stories would have Peter finishing his round putting with his driver or his sand wedge or something. It dawned on me that if Peter fired me—which he should have, by all rights—I'd never find work on that tour again. My whole dream—to caddie my way to Scotland—was suddenly in jeopardy, to say nothing of the precarious balance of our financial existence, thousands of miles from home, which we had left with a big send-off party. Even if we returned home, my newspaper job wasn't available to me for another year. *I had signed papers, legal documents!* I couldn't get any air into my lungs. How was I going to explain to my wife of four months that I was a caddie failure! Stifling heat surged through my body. I wanted to sink into the soft Mediterranean soil. Peter said nothing. I could only imagine what he was thinking.

I don't know how I lost the club. Either it bounced out of the bag while I was running or I never put it back in the bag after the exchange of clubs under the tree. At that point, I figured only one of two things could happen. Either Peter would sack me, or I would improve. Worse was not possible.

CHAPTER THREE

Locomotion

I MANAGED TO GO BLUNDER-FREE in the third and fourth rounds of the Mediterranean Open, and when I asked Peter what time to meet him for the start of week two—the Balearic Islands Open on the island of Majorca, one hundred and twenty miles off the east coast of Spain—he didn't say don't bother. So late on the Sunday night after the tournament, my wife and I, along with forty other caddies and a dozen players, flocked to the St. Raphael train station to catch the overnight train to Spain. No food till Port Bou.

The Mediterranean Open had concluded in mid-afternoon and the train out of town didn't depart until nearly midnight; caddie wallets were stuffed with post-tournament cash and the bars were open. These facts did not promote tranquility. When I saw an English-speaking caddie sticking his off-centered nose in the thin face of a French-speaking station official—they were debating the fine points of the open container law—I prayed that he would not be in our compartment.

My prayers were answered. Christine and I were in the same car as the barrister-caddie, but four or five compartments down. When we pushed open the door to our computer-assigned quarters, we found that the two lower bunks and the floor space in between them had already been claimed. A young professional golfer, an Englishman named Steve Bottomley, was on the left bunk, and his brother and caddie, Ian, was on the right. Sleeping on the floor in between them was the Bottomley golf bag encased in a canvas travel pouch. It looked like a gigantic cocoon. We shoved in our luggage, and my golf bag, and climbed in.

"How'd you go?" Steve asked me. He saw my bag and assumed that I was a player. He wanted to know how I had fared at the Mediterranean.

"I'm a caddie," I said.

"Traveling with your golf bag," Steve said skeptically.

"That's right."

"And your wife."

"Right."

"Are you sure you're not on holiday?"

I was quite sure of that. Problems at work consumed my thoughts.

There was conversation for a while, but the Bottomleys and Christine were asleep before the train was an hour out of St. Raphael. For me, sleep was impossible. The week's numbers kept running through my head. Teravainen had shot 69-75-72-74, a total of 290 strokes, six over par. He finished in a tie for twenty-ninth place, the middle of the pack, and won £3,540, which in February of 1991 was worth $7,000. (The Gulf War had weakened the dollar overseas; in late February, a pound was equal to nearly two dollars.) Ian Woosnam won the tournament and £66,000 by taking eleven fewer shots than Peter over the seventy-two holes. In my mind, I had no trouble slicing twelve shots off Peter's four-day score. Given another chance, he might have made a certain three-foot putt. Given another chance, balls driven into trees, onto rocks, and into streams, might have found fairways. Given better fortune, shots that bounced off hillocks and into bunkers might have bounced onto greens. This is the optimism upon which all golf is rooted.

I am optimistic by nature. Still, I wondered if I would have a job after Majorca. I knew Peter had to make the cut there if I were to have a chance of staying on his bag. Teravainen was a journeyman. In more than eleven years of professional golf, representing hundreds of tournaments, he had never won an event on any of the four major golf tours in the world: the U. S. tour, the European tour, the Japanese tour, and the Australian tour. His dream was to win one. His reality was that he made his living by making thirty-six-hole cuts. In 1990, Peter had entered thirty-one tournaments and made the cut in only eighteen of them. If you don't make the cut, you don't make a paycheck. Expenses are all out of pocket. The cutthroat, Darwinian capitalism of tournament golf was immensely appealing to Peter. Shoot score X, make amount Y. Peter ate numbers. He studied stock market tables. He studied racing forms. He had cut scores calculated long before tournament officials did. He had majored in Economics at Yale and he valued numerical analyses. But he believed in charms, too. I felt that if he made the cut in Majorca—*"two in a row with Bamberger; not bad"*—he wouldn't be so quick to dismiss me. That was my hope, anyway.

I did not put up a brave front for Christine. In the trough of our bed in St. Raphael, I had told her about the missing 7-iron, and about giving Peter the wrong ball. She knew my employment status was precarious. She was supportive. She never said, "Oh—I have married a caddie incompetent!" She told me not to worry. She said she could start a golf tour laundry service. Or a traveling tour barber shop. She said we'd get by.

I looked at her on the train's bouncing bunk bed. Its scratchy sheets did not bother her in the slightest. She was sleeping soundly, contentedly. As the train hurtled through the night and past the hamlets of coastal France, I enjoyed the simple fact that my wife and I were sharing sleeping quarters with strangers. We were traveling loose. Our married life was off to an adventurous start.

I was afraid to go to sleep. The Bottomleys had warned us that thieving was common on overnight trains. They were sleeping with their pants on, and with their passports, watches, and wallets stuffed in their front pockets. Ian Bottomley, I noticed, didn't even risk taking off his expensive cowboy boots before retiring.

In the middle of the night, I saw those cowboy boots revolve one hundred and eighty degrees, from heel up to toe up, and Ian—somehow sensing that I was awake and still reliving the strokes of the Mediterranean Open—suddenly asked, "So how'd your man go this week?"

I was pleased to have somebody with whom to talk, but for a moment I felt a conversational stymie: I could not regard Teravainen as my *man.* A caddie's man is his regular boss. The itinerant caddie has a *bag.* As in, "Whose bag you on this week?" By using the word *man*, Ian was paying me a compliment. He had assumed my job was steady. I didn't want to bore him with the small traumas of my professional life, so I said, "Tied for twenty-ninth. How'd you guys do?" In the language of caddies, *you guys* has an even higher standing than your man; you guys suggests that the caddie and the player are a single entity.

"Fortieth," Ian said. "Didn't make a putt, didn't hit a fairway."

I asked Ian how long he was out for. A tour caddie is *out,* until he returns home for more traditional work. Ian said his plan was to caddie for his brother for as long as the British economy slumbered. He had ambivalent feelings about the job, though. "Of all the arts," he said, "caddying's the most frustrating."

I asked him why.

"There's nothing really you can do for your man. You realize that at the end of the day. You can give him good yardages, tell him how you see the knobs of the greens, is it uphill, is it downhill, all that. You can throw your grass clippings in the air until the sky falls down, tell him the direction of the breeze and how hard it's blowing. You can warn him that he's got a flier lie or that the green is as hard as a motorway or that the pin position is for suckers only. You can make all the calculations, do all your considering. You can put the club in his hand, tell him to hit the soft six or the hard seven. But you cannot take the bloody swing for him."

I told Ian I wouldn't want to hit any shot for my bossman.

"I would," Ian said. "I play off two. When I'm playing well, I can beat Steve. I know his tendencies, his weaknesses. If the wind is blowing a certain way, if the ball is sitting a certain way, if it's a shot I know he's not comfortable with, I'd take that shot. Sometimes in a tournament I can predict the exact outcome of the shot before he makes it. When it's just the two of us in a friendly bounce game, he's more likely to make these stunning shots that just amaze you. That's because when we play at home there's no analysis. You just take in the shot: your eyes tell your head what to do, your head tells your body, and your body makes the shot. It's easy. In practice rounds before the tournament, same thing. It's the analysis that kills you. Once a tournament starts, it's like, 'OK, where's my left knee supposed to be at impact?' Who cares? How are you going to feel the shot when you're worried about the position of your left knee at impact?"

I listened attentively. Christine continued to sleep. So did Steve. The train roared on, Spain-bound. I suggested to Ian that maybe these seemingly minor technical swing fascinations were critical to success at a certain level of the game, that they gave the top player something manageable on which to blame success or failure.

"That's a theory," Ian said. That meant he didn't agree. "The thing with golf is that some people take to it like a fish to water and some people never figure it out. Anybody who's playing on one of the four major tours, they took to the game straight off. By the time these guys are old enough to get in a pub, they have *swings,* good, mature swings, swings with personalities all their own. Once the swing is developed, it doesn't change much. The magazines get all this yardage out of how David Leadbetter did a complete remake of Nick Faldo's swing, and that's how Faldo was able to twice win our Open and twice win your Masters in the space of three years. What are they talking about? The plane of his swing got a tiny bit flatter. That's it. The main thing is the head. Is it off? Is it on? His is obviously on. He's got good thoughts going. I guarantee you that when he's on the golf course standing over his ball he's thinking only about executing the shot the way he wants to execute it. He's seeing the overall shot, the overall swing that's going to produce it, not a bunch of little pieces. Must be, or he wouldn't be making the shots he's making. That's the thing about Nicklaus. He started this idea of standing behind the ball and seeing in your mind's eye the entire shot before you get going. Now everybody does it. But a lot of players just go through the motions, they're not really seeing it. They're thinking, 'Do I have my left knee in the right position at impact,' or, 'Will that sponsor come through,' or, 'Does my shirt match my sweater.' People say Faldo's aloof on the golf course. You'd be aloof too if your brain was flooded with pictures like his is. This is high-level stuff, what Faldo's doing. People are so quick to dismiss it because they don't like his personality. They think he's a robot. They don't get it. He's made a breakthrough. There's probably only one level of golf higher than what Faldo is doing. I don't even know if this highest level is attainable, least not on a regular basis."

This is the nature of golf conversation. You start off with something simple. *How'd you guys do?* Soon you're hiking in the brain's most inaccessible hills. Highest level, higher than what Faldo is doing? "What, what is it?" I asked eagerly.

Ian didn't answer right away, and for a moment I was afraid that he wouldn't answer at all. Some people—Hogan among them, I believe—know certain secret things about the game that they don't want to reveal, not out of selfishness, but out of a fear that once the idea is spoken, it will be stripped of its validity, because no one else will understand it. In time, Ian Bottomley answered.

"You've probably experienced it, here and there. I have. The highest level is to be standing over your ball, playing your shot, and to be thinking about nothing at all." He paused. "Think about it," Ian said.

And with that, he spun around again and returned to sleep, leaving me in the dust of our perplexing little talk. What do you think about to think about nothing? And what was it that he said, that by the time you're old enough to get into a pub, your swing has a personality of its own? Does that mean if you're twenty-one years old—or, in my case, thirty-one years old—and your swing is still badly flawed your chances for improvement are improbable? If that is true, I thought, my game is in trouble. Can a swing really have a personality? I supposed that it could: some swings are jumpy, some are lazy, some are efficient, some are wasteful, some look good but accomplish little, some look ugly but are effective. Peter's swing was loaded with personality. My own had elements of a personality—rushed and tense. But were those the fundamental elements of my personality? I didn't think so; I hoped not. What happens if your personality is poorly suited to golf? Do you have to develop a personality well-suited to golf to become good at golf? Can you change your personality? What type of person am I, anyhow? Do I reveal my true self through my golf? My head swam. Finally, I felt drowsy. The train pushed forward.

CHAPTER FOUR

MAKING CUTS

I WAS TRAVELING ON TWO PASSPORTS: a caddie's passport, which let me into the locker rooms and the caddie yards, and a reporter's passport, which let me into the clubhouses and the press tents. This dual citizenship proved handy at the Balearic Islands Open, on the Spanish island of Majorca. The tournament was run by a company called Amen Corner, which is owned by Seve Ballesteros. I wanted to get near Seve. That was a goal. But in Spain, golf is still a rich man's game and at Spanish tournaments caddie movements are closely guarded. It was only the press badge that allowed me near The Great Man.

That is what golf fans throughout Europe, including Great Britain and Ireland, call Ballesteros. The Spaniard's impact on world golf has never been fully appreciated in the United States, where he is regarded as an enigma. For the most part, the American golf fan sees Ballesteros only at the British Open, at the Masters, and, in odd-numbered years, at the Ryder Cup, the biennial match-play golf competition in which top American professionals play top European professionals for a jug. He is nearly always a force in those three affairs, the Masters and the British Open because the venues suit his style of play, and the Ryder Cup because the format does: he loves going tête-à-tête;

it gets his blood stirring. Ballesteros, who would play more frequently in the United States if the rules of the U. S. tour weren't so resistant to foreigners, competes in the two other major golf championships, the United States Open and the Professional Golfers' Association of America Championship. But he doesn't often fare well in them. They are typically played on courses that are too grassy for him to make the kinds of shots he loves. Ballesteros's game is based on creativity. He *likes* missing fairways, he *likes* missing greens; in scrambling he is forced to be inventive. At the U. S. Open and at the P. G. A. Championship, accuracy is prized above all else. Typically, if you miss fairways and greens in those championships, you make bogeys. That's because just off the fairways and just off the greens, there is lots of over-fertilized and over-watered grass, long and thick and unplayable. At most of the British Open venues the fairways are reasonably generous and the territories neighboring the greens are closely-mown; it's the humps, the hollows, the bunkers, and the changing winds that cause all the hair-pulling. The golf course of the Augusta National Golf Club, in Augusta, Georgia, where the Masters is played each April, is the same. It has lots of trees, but no rough. When the world-class player misses greens and fairways in the Masters, he can attempt recovery with almost any shot in his repertoire. When you drive it into the rough at the U. S. Open or at the P. G. A. Championship, in most years, you take out your sand wedge and slash at your ball, hoping to move it to the fairway. This is not the Ballesteros way.

I came of golf age as a teenager in the mid-1970s and one of the first extraordinary shots I think I remember—either I actually remember it or I've heard it described so often that I think I remember it—came at the seventy-second hole of the British Open at Royal Birkdale in 1976. Ballesteros was nineteen then (the same age as my three-years-older brother), and had led the championship for the first three rounds. During the fourth round he wavered, the way tournament-long front runners invariably do. He came to the par-five home hole needing a four to finish as the joint runner-up, with Nicklaus. He crushed two shots and was faced with an unnerving third, a hybrid shot that was neither a pitch nor a chip. It required an invention: he had to carry two bunkers and land the ball on a tiny island of hard ground, then use the contours of a little bump in front of the green to maneuver his ball to the pin. In the end, he pitched with a chipping club —the shot was a golfing sphinx—and he left himself four feet for the bird. He had total will over his golf ball. He holed the putt. He tied Nicklaus. Even though Johnny Miller won, Ballesteros carried the day.

Three years later, in 1979, he won the British Open, his first major title. With the trophy of the world's oldest golf championship in hand, Ballesteros claimed the victory not only for himself, his family, and his country, but also for all of Europe. When the Ryder Cup came to the Greenbrier, in West Virginia, in September of that year, the visiting team was called "Europe"; its previous name, "Great Britain and Ireland," had become extinct. The borders of the team had been expanded to accommodate The Great Man.

During the 1980s, Ballesteros won two more British Open championships, in 1984 and in 1988. In 1980 he became the first European to win the Masters, which he won again in 1983. Seve was no Hogan, no golfing machine—his game was erratic and did not stand up to acute tests of accuracy. But he was thrilling to watch. Even on TV, you could sense the aura around him.

The thing about him that intrigued me most was that he often seemed to be on the verge of happiness, but he never seemed truly satisfied. Maybe this is the trademark of the genuine artist. When he made stunning shots, his face, which hides nothing, said, "This is what I do." When he played good shots that went unrewarded his face said, "Who dares to conspire against me?" When he played shots poorly his face said, "The next shot goes in." His victories seemed to bring him contentment, but never wild glee.

On the day before the start of the Balearic Islands Open, I found Ballesteros in a pressroom, set up in the basement of the modern and *grande* clubhouse of the Santa Ponsa Golf Club. He was a strikingly handsome man, with shiny hair and dark skin and bright eyes. He was talking to Spanish reporters. The questions were long and his answers were short. Sipping an orange soda, he continually looked at his Rolex watch. The proceedings lacked the graciousness that one finds when, say, the American press interviews Nicklaus. When the reporters were through with him and he was through with them, I approached Ballesteros. Even though he was to me an exalted figure, I was only slightly nervous. Had I been caddying in Seve's group, I would have been very nervous. Had I been in a gallery, watching him trying to disentangle himself from a predicament with a title on the line, I would have been very nervous. But interviewing is at the heart of my real profession, and asking questions always has a calming effect for me. I asked if the Spanish press treated him differently from reporters in other parts of the world. He said they did. "The Spanish press, they always expect me to win," he said, speaking English nearly perfectly, but with a charming Continental accent. "They think I should win every time I play. If I don't, they write headlines, 'Ballesteros's Game in Trouble.' "

Ballesteros's game was in trouble. The previous year, 1990, the year he became a father, had been a professional disaster for him: one lone win, at the Balearic Islands Open, his own tournament. The season was his least fruitful since 1975, when he had still been learning the game as an eighteen-year-old touring professional. (The son of a farmer, Ballesteros quit school at fourteen to caddie, turned professional at sixteen, and started playing the tour at seventeen. In Europe, that's not so uncommon; very few players on the European tour continued school past the age of eighteen.) He followed a banner year in 1988—the year he married Carmen Botín, the Brown-educated daughter of a socially and financially prominent Spanish banking family—with an uneven year in 1989. Then 1990 was, by Ballesteros's standards, a golfing fiasco. Some people wondered if he had lost his motivation. He certainly had not played with his customary élan. I asked him if he was enjoying the game.

"I never enjoy the game when I'm not playing well," he said. "Do you?"

"No," I said.

Ballesteros hunched his shoulders, put his palms up in the air, and raised his dark, thick eyebrows.

I asked him, "Do you still have the magic?" He did not find the question cryptic or bizarre. He got it immediately.

"Yes," he said. "But I don't know where it is."

And with that, he walked to the practice tee, seeking to straighten out his problems, the physical manifestation of which was a strong tendency to hook shots.

As soon as he started hitting shots, he was surrounded by other touring professionals, both well-established and obscure. Some wanted to study his method, to watch him and smell him and examine the direction and depth of his divots, hoping to find something that they could apply to themselves. Ballesteros had, after all, won sixty tournaments since 1976. Others wanted to offer him advice, hoping to be the man to return Ballesteros to form. A player from England named Derrick Cooper kept pointing to Ballesteros's feet. A player from Fiji named Vijay Singh kept pointing to Ballesteros's left hand. Ballesteros's willingness to listen was not surprising, for in golf one never knows where a breakthrough might lurk.

Successful golf requires luck, too, something to make you feel that the supernatural is on your side. In the final round of Ballesteros's first British Open victory, at Royal Lytham and St. Annes in 1979, he hit only two fairways yet almost always found his ball sitting kindly. On the sixteenth, he hit a long slice and his ball finished in a parking field, under a car. He received a free drop and came up again with a nice lie. It is not unreasonable to think that all the good fortune of that day lingered within Ballesteros in the years that followed and contributed to a sense of fearlessness.

In the second round in Majorca in 1991, Ballesteros had unexpected good fortune again. After an opening round of 73, he came to the last three holes needing a birdie and two pars just to make the thirty-six-hole cut. Players like Teravainen, who struggle week to week to make a living, face this kind of oppression routinely, but for Ballesteros surviving a cut is seldom an issue. There was no doubt that making the cut was important to him. As the tournament host and defending champion, he would have to spend the weekend at the club even if he wasn't playing, which would have meant hearing a great many people asking him what was wrong with his game. When he hit his second shot into the pond protecting the green on the sixteenth, his chances of playing on Saturday and Sunday appeared to have sunk, along with his ball.

But the island of Majorca was enduring a severe water shortage, and the pond turned out to be manmade, and those facts saved Seve: the bottom of the pond was made of cement and there wasn't much water in it. Seve's ball hit a shallow spot, bounced out, and onto the green. He made his birdie and he made his cut, right on the button. He played poorly again on Saturday, a 78, but on Sunday he turned in the best score of the day, a 68, and for the first time in a long time Ballesteros had cause for hope. He came off the course saying, "I must play more golf, I must play more golf."

Peter had his hands full in Majorca, too. In the first round there, he had the bad fortune to draw a late-afternoon tee time. The morning players played under sunny skies and in warm air. Even when Peter began, the sky was pale, the winds were calm, and the air was temperate. But within an hour after his first tee shot, the sky turned a peculiar brownish-gray and the temperature fell about forty degrees, nearly to freezing. A fierce wind arrived. A sandstorm from North Africa—what the islanders called *la viento calima*—had swept over Majorca. You could feel the misting sand against your cheeks. A thin layer of sand gathered in the lines on your forehead and tears collected in your eyes. The wind and the cold made it impossible to hold steady over putts. The Santa Ponsa Golf Club course, already long, difficult, and rough around the edges, became longer and more difficult and even rougher around the edges. The climate was scary and dramatic and concentrating on golf was difficult. The merry band of sun-seeking British tourists who had been following Brian Barnes—Peter's playing partner for rounds one and two and a European tour star in the 1970s who defeated Nicklaus twice in one day in the 1975 Ryder Cup matches—had dwindled away to nothing. This was weather in which Barnes, a showy Scot, was able to demonstrate his marvelous shot-making ability, but he had an audience of only two. When he stepped into a deep fairway bunker with a bulky-headed 3-wood to attempt a shot few modern pros would dare, Peter said to me, "Watch this—the old pro's gonna manufacture something here." Barnes picked the ball clean and got it over the bunker's three-foot lip with a foot to spare. Peter and I watched the ball fly, low and true, through the brownish-gray sky and the thirty-knot, sand-carrying breeze for over two hundred yards. It was a superb play, but there was no gallery to applaud Barnes's artistry.

Considering the conditions, Peter's 75 in the opening Thursday round was a good score, but a golf tournament scoreboard makes no allowances for changing weather conditions and the morning scores, in more benign conditions, had been low. Peter studied the board, which listed every player and showed the number of strokes taken by each player on each hole. (There's no place to hide in tournament golf.) By the overall standards of the day, his 75 was not a good score. After some calculating, Teravainen figured he would need a 73 in Friday's round to qualify for weekend play, and a paycheck. Making the cut was as important to me as it was to Peter. The sandstorm from North Africa had cost Peter a couple of shots, and hadn't helped me a bit, either.

By the time Peter reached the sixteenth hole on Friday, the hole where Ballesteros had bounced out of the cement-bottomed pond, he knew he had to close his round with three pars to make the cut. For a player of Teravainen's caliber, there is normally nothing difficult about making three consecutive pars. But having to make three straight pars to survive a cut is a different matter. You cannot help but think about money. The expenses for the week are the same, paycheck or no paycheck. Without three pars, the balance sheet for the week would be bright red. Watching Peter sweat, I was reminded of what a tough racket tournament golf is.

It wasn't that long ago that players on the U. S. tour thought in terms of survival. Right through the mid-1980s, that was the prevalent thought. Most players did not have private benefactors and three top-ten finishes could not cover a year's worth of expenses. In the United States, those days are gone. Beginning in about 1986, corporate America decided, *en masse*, that the U. S. golf tour mirrored its own Reagan-era image: independent, financially successful, conservative, well-mannered. Led by Nabisco, corporations started investing in the game in unprecedented sums. The influx of money made the tour even more financially successful, more conservative, and more corporate-feeling. A tournament known as the The Crosby (for Bing) since its birth in 1937 became, in 1986, the AT&T Pebble Beach National Pro-Am. From 1986 through 1990, the size of the average purse at a U. S. tour event nearly doubled, to the point where it wasn't necessary to be an exceptional player to make an exceptional living. The idea of the touring professional as wily entrepreneur was nearly dead.

On the European tour—where there is less money and where fewer players have benefactors, and where most players turn professional as teenagers and have nothing else on which to fall back—the journeyman obsession with survival remains prevalent. The obsession is not only about financial survival; it's about playing well enough to keep playing. That's what Peter wanted.

The hole on the sixteenth was cut just over the cement pond, but Peter did not flirt with it: his approach shot flew over the green, his chip shot was short, and when he holed a six-footer for par we were both relieved. On the seventeenth, a short par-four curving to the left, Peter grunted after hitting a mammoth Whiplash drive. His partner, Brian Barnes, was impressed. He looked at Peter and said, "If you don't make some money this year, my ass is a dumpling." He was trying to relax Peter. Barnes's father-in-law, the late Max Faulkner, winner of the 1951 British Open, believed that the professional golfer had a responsibility to make the game look effortless to the golfing public, regardless of his internal turmoil. Barnes adopted that credo. He created a skirt-chasing *bon vivant* persona for himself. He wore tight-fitting orange trousers and enormous tinted glasses with heavy black frames. On occasion, he'd mark his ball with a beer can and ask attractive women in his gallery to recommend to him a good masseuse. This was his way of addressing the suffocating tension of tournament golf.

Peter could not be so loose. He fought tension with intensity. As he struggled to make the cut in Majorca, his lips were dry and his forehead was perspiring. His wife was pregnant, they were looking to buy a house, and he needed to make money. As he prepared to play a short, delicate pitch to the seventeenth green, his knuckles were white. He struck the ball tentatively, and it came up short. Barnes was only two shots off the lead, but he knew precisely where Teravainen stood, what Peter had to do to make the cut. He said, "C'mon, Pete, hit the thing." He knew what Peter was enduring; he was rooting for *survival.* Peter chipped to three feet on seventeen and made the putt squarely.

On the eighteenth green, Peter faced another three-footer for par. His stroke was wobbly and the ball was headed straight for the left lip. Luckily for Peter, and for me, the cup was sloppily cut and the left lip had an inward lean. When the ball settled at the bottom of the hole, Peter pointed his head up, wiped his forehead, and exhaled audibly. He extended a hand to Barnes.

"Thanks for the game," Peter said to him. "Play well on the weekend."

And Barnes said, "You, too, Pete."

Teravainen had made the cut, and I knew that meant I had a chance of sticking.

You may have noticed that in describing my work for Peter I have avoided the pronoun *we,* which caddies have been using for generations to assume partial credit for the accomplishments of their players. I've omitted the word because for those first six competitive rounds, the four at the Mediterranean Open and the first two at the Balearic Islands Open, I was in no true sense a caddie. I was, and this is the most pejorative label in all of caddying, a bag carrier. My goal was to be a real caddie.

In any player-caddie relationship, the player (who is the employer, no matter what some caddies would have you believe) must set the tone. Ultimately, the player must decide if there will be chit-chat between shots, or if there will be discussions about what club to hit, or what line to take. In the end, the player determines if the caddie is a servant (*Give me the driver*) or an adviser (*Is the breeze helping or hurting us?*) or something in between. I wanted very much to be involved, but I had to wait for Peter to decide when it was time for me to participate. Sometime during the third round in Majorca, he decided it was time. What prompted him, I do not know.

My first involution was exceedingly minor, but I regarded it as a breakthrough. On the fifth green, Peter and both of his playing partners, an Australian named Wayne Riley and an Englishman named Robert Lee, had putts of nearly identical length. The rules of golf require that the player whose ball is farthest from the hole plays first. When I went to the hole to remove the flagstick, Peter said to me, "Who's away?" It wasn't much, but it was the first question he had asked me that required any sort of judgment. Answering required an understanding of rule 10.2 in the Rules of Golf regarding the order of play, and the competence to administer it.

"It's Wayne, then you, then Robert," I said.

"OK," Peter said.

Not dramatic stuff, I realize, but important to me at the time.

I must have handled the task satisfactorily, because on the eighth tee Peter asked me a more involved question. The eighth was a par-four of 385 yards with a stream running across the fairway 290 yards away from the back of the tee. With Peter's length, any shot with a wood could fetch the stream, yet it was desirable to have the tee shot finish as near to the stream as possible, to leave the shortest possible distance for the approach shot into the small green. As Peter stared down the hole, he said to me, "1-iron or 2?"

It was the moment for which I had been waiting. On every shot from our start together, I had tried to prepare myself for anything he might ask. My time had arrived, and I was ready.

I had grass clippings in my fingers and gently I set the blades free—no heavy-handed toss. I could see that there was a good draft with us. During the first two rounds, the wind had been in the opposite direction. The hole was downhill. The fairway was hard and running. Long was bad. I said, "Hit the two."

Peter pulled the 2-iron from the bag and hit it well. The ball finished about seven yards short of the stream, in the middle of the fairway. He said nothing, but I knew he was pleased. The 1-iron would have been too much, it would have put him in the stream. I felt a certain satisfaction: I had influenced positively a shot executed by a professional golfer playing for his livelihood. I had played a role, albeit a tiny one, in helping Peter do his job better.

Peter was starting to show faith in me. On the tenth tee, he took one of his Whiplash swings, complete with a grunt and a double follow-through. While the ball sailed to a distant land, hanging in the air for at least five or six seconds and carrying more than three hundred yards with a sweeping right-to-left arc, there was time enough for a conversation.

"So that's the Whiplash," Wayne Riley said. The ball continued to soar and everybody watched it.

"You've heard of it," Peter said. I could not tell if he was flattered.

"The Whiplash, the Singapore Sling—it's infamous," the Australian said. The ball landed.

As we came off the tee, Peter said to me, discreetly and seriously, "I don't want people expecting me to make that swing. I'm not trying to entertain anybody; that swing just comes out sometimes. If people say to you, 'Peter still doing the Whiplash?' just say that I'm driving the ball nicely. Enough of this Whiplash business." Peter didn't want to be regarded as some sort of golfing freak show. He was asking me to help in public relations.

Peter had rough finishes on both Saturday and Sunday in Majorca. On Saturday, after starting with two birdies, he played the next fifteen holes in level par and had a two-foot par putt on the last for a solid two-under-par round. Just as he brought his putter head back on the two-footer, a ball machine on the driving range dropped hundreds of golf balls into a metal bin, creating a startling thunder, and Peter missed the putt. Given that kind of memory of the hole, I wasn't surprised when Peter missed from eighteen inches on the eighteenth on Sunday, for a dismal 76.

I wondered if the final round would do in our partnership; I was worried. Then, after we sealed up his bag for the next trip, he said casually, "I'll see you first thing Tuesday morning at Tarragona." Tarragona, Spain, was the site for week three, the Catalonia Open. I had a job. In Majorca, Peter, Seve, and I had all made the cut.

After his closing 68 in Majorca, and after coming off the eighteenth green saying, "I must play more golf, I must play more golf," Ballesteros made a call and became a last-minute entrant in the Catalonia Open. The Masters was a month away and Ballesteros wanted to get his game in shape.

Ballesteros had begun the new season with a new caddie, a boyish-looking, pale-skinned, hollow-eyed Englishman named Billy Foster. Ballesteros went through caddies quickly and works them hard—even his brothers never lasted long on his bag—so if Foster was nervous about his new job, I certainly could sympathize with him. In Tarragona, I heard Foster describe the inherent difficulty of carrying for The Great Man.

"We're playing the first, the par-five with the water? He hits a decent tee shot. He's got 270 to the pin, 245 to carry the pond. The lie is kind of tight. I'm thinking, 'Lay up with a 4-iron and pitch on.' It's not like he's hitting the ball that great. He says, 'Driver?' And I'm thinking, 'Who am I to tell Seve he can't hit a driver off a tight lie when he's got a 245-yard carry?' " Foster's audience of caddies in the back of a bus nodded sympathetically. Ballesteros hit driver, thinly, and knocked his ball in the water.

When I heard that story, I had a strong feeling that Ballesteros was in for a spectacular year, one way or the other.

In Tarragona, I became a real caddie. At the Catalonia Open, Peter asked me to start recording certain pieces of information in my yardage book—a slim notebook that shows a map of each hole and the distances from various markers to the fronts of the greens. He wanted me to note the distance he hit each shot, the club he used, and the direction and strength of the wind. He wanted the information to make club selection more scientific. For example, during the second round in Tarragona, he hit a 4-iron 191 yards into a ten-knot breeze on the par-three fifth. I wrote that down in the book. Later in the round, on the par-four twelfth, he faced a 193-yard approach shot into a ten-knot wind. He asked, "Isn't this shot like the one on five? What'd I hit there?" And I reminded him what he had done on the fifth. He was secure when he pulled out the 4-iron; he knew it was the right club. I was surprised Peter wanted all this information. Despite his off-course number crunching, he was, in the main, a feel player, not a technician. He was a man who believed in lucky numbers. But if this information added to his confidence, it could only help. I was glad to have the extra responsibility.

The system had a breaking point, we soon discovered. In the fourth round of the Catalonia Open, the elements threw all our figuring out of whack. That round was played on a bright blue, chilly spring day, with the wind blowing at forty and fifty knots straight across the treeless golf course (a promising, but new and raw, Robert Trent Jones, Jr., course called Club de Bonmont-Terres Noves, in the rocky, hilly, arid farm country of Mont Roig Del Camp, about twenty-five miles from downtown Tarragona and five miles from the Mediterranean Sea). On the practice tee, the metal buckets that hold balls skittered across the practice field, looking like those airboats used in the Everglades. Golf bags propped up carefully against walls of the clubhouse fell seconds later. Visors flew off heads. The flapping noise of wind-breakers filled the air; you could barely hear the person next to you speak. Walking uphill and into the wind, with the forty-pound bag on your back, you felt like you needed a push. If you drove the ball 190 yards into the wind you had crushed it. There was a par-four hole that took two woods and a middle iron to reach, even for long hitters.

At the start of the day, Peter said, "Today will show you who can play golf." He shot a three-under-par 69. Nobody scored better. We moved from thirty-first place after three rounds to a tie for twelfth place. After the round, people came up to Peter and said, "Good one." Caddies came up to me and said, "You guys shot *what?*" It was Peter's best finish in a European tour event in twenty-one months, and I felt I had made a contribution. I was a bag-carrier no longer. I was a caddie.

On the par-three eighth, Peter had 203 yards to the pin, with a pond in front of the green. The hole was straight downwind and Peter could not believe what he was thinking.

"Eight or a nine?" he said to me. In normal conditions, Peter hits his 8-iron about 155 yards.

"Nine," I said.

"All right," Peter said, resigned. His voice seemed to say, *I can't believe it, but if you say so.* He knocked the ball stiff. That was great fun.

CHAPTER FIVE

CADDIE OMNIBUS

TURNBERRY GEORGE, an organizer of the caddie bus, told me that there was only one cheap, efficient way to get from Tarragona, Spain, to Oporto, Portugal, site of the Portuguese Open, and that, of course, was on his caddie bus. The train, he said, would take twenty-four hours and my wallet would be stolen. A hire car, he said, would cost three hundred pounds with gas and tolls and would dismantle on Portugal's rugged back roads and nobody would come to help. A flight, he said, was out of the question. The caddie bus, he said, was the way to go. There would even be a movie on it. That's what he said.

A few minutes after the final putts of the Catalonia Open had been holed (José-María Olazábal ran away with the tournament), Turnberry George's bus, with fifty-eight caddies, one caddie spouse (Christine), and one player (Teravainen), headed out and for the open road. I had been told that the price for the trip would be about thirty pounds, but it turned out to be fifty. I had been told that the bus would be about half-filled, but it turned out to be packed. I had been told that smoking would be restricted to the back, but the two drivers turned out to be chain smokers. No matter. Peter (and I) had just concluded a superb round of golf and the happy glow of that would last for a long time. Looking back, I think the feeling survived until about seven hours into the trip. That was when Turnberry George tried to show his movie, which damn near caused a riot.

For the first couple hundred miles or so, when we were nearing Madrid, things were peaceful. The day's winds had made everybody weary. A Pink Floyd album, *The Wall,* was played again and again on the bus's tape deck, and the music, at once melodic and psychedelic, had a lulling effect. Before long, Pink Floyd was backed by a chorus of open-mouthed caddies snoring away.

I was eager to figure out how much money Peter, and I, had won. Because Peter tied for twelfth with seven others, figuring his share of the purse took some calculating. (We had left before the official tabulations had been made.) Solo twelfth place would have paid £5,160, but the eight-way tie changed the numbers significantly. You had to add the twelfth-place money with the money for thirteenth, fourteenth, fifteenth, sixteenth, seventeenth, eighteenth, and nineteenth, and then divide by eight. I tallied up the numbers with a scorecard pencil, performed the division, and said to Teravainen, who was sitting across the aisle from me, "You know how much we won this week? Four thousand, three hundred and fifty-seven pounds."

"And fifty pence," Peter said. He was right. I had neglected the fifty pence.

Peter, by his reckoning and everybody else's, was the most frugal player on the European tour. While most of the players were flying to Oporto by way of London or Madrid (except about a half-dozen Spanish players, their girlfriends, and their wives, who were driving in a caravan of cars), Teravainen was on the caddie bus, and pleased to be. In Majorca, he had chided me for staying in a thirty-five-dollar-a-night apartment complex, where most of the caddies were—he had found a place for half that. Some people thought Peter would play better if he spent more money, but he failed to see any logic in that. He had two rules about room and board: never skip a meal to save money and never sleep on a bed that will hurt your back. Aside from that, pretty much anything would do. At every tour stop, he knew the locations of the all-you-can-eat cafeterias and he guarded closely the names of certain bed-and-breakfasts, hostels, and one-star hotels that he frequented year after year. But he never stayed in tents and it had been years since he had slept in a van, as Ian Woosnam did in his early years on the tour and as some caddies continued to do. (A few caddies stayed in tents, too, using their rain suits as pajamas.) Anyway, it was mostly caddies who thought Peter needed to spend more money. And that was because there were very few players on the tour who paid a lower caddie wage than Peter.

At first, I found that hard to believe. When Peter began paying me I didn't think too many players could be more generous. (That was before I learned about the Swedes.) He gave me two hundred pounds per week for the first two weeks, and at Tarragona, when my position became more secure, he gave me a twenty-five-pound raise. (The salary often was paid in the equivalent of pounds in local money, or in a combination of currencies that anticipated upcoming currency needs. One month into the journey, I had American dollars, British pounds, French francs, Spanish pesetas, Portuguese escudos, and Italian liras jumbled in my wallet, and my change purse weighed a kilo or two.) In addition to my salary, I received a bonus based on a percentage of Peter's winnings. This bonus was not a tip, but a fundamental part of caddie compensation, without which the concept of the tour caddie would not exist as we know it. It is because the caddie's net worth is affected by every shot his player makes that the caddie stays involved in every shot. The system nearly guarantees that the interests of the player and caddie coincide. (Every so often, you get a caddie who grows to dislike his player so much that he roots for him to fail.)

Peter defined my bonus as five percent of his post-tax winnings. In Spain, the government took twenty-five percent of a player's winnings, regardless of nationality, and the European tour always deducted two-and-a-half percent for its operating costs, which Peter regarded as a tax. So to calculate my Catalonia Open bonus, I had to reduce £4,357.50 by 27.5 percent and then take five percent of that. Peter's net income on £4,357.50

after taxes was £3,159 (rounding off to the nearest pound) and five percent of that was £158. With my salary, I had earned £383 for the week. That translated to about $700; the pound was worth $1.85 in mid-March 1991.

I then tried to figure how far our £383 had taken us. We had hitched a ride from Barcelona to Tarragona with an American named Tim Kelly, Ping's European tour rep, and he would take no money for gas; we stayed at one of the caddie hotels, Hotel Le Cirque, in the heart of old Tarragona, for six nights at twenty pounds per night; we ate most of our dinners at a place called Mistral Pizzeria for about twelve pounds per night; we saw Francis Ford Coppola's *Padrino II,* in English with Spanish subtitles, at a Tarragona revival movie house for six pounds; I bought a pair of brown corduroy trousers for twelve pounds (I had come over with two pairs of khakis and two pairs of dungarees, but was told immediately that caddying in blue jeans was prohibited by the European Tour Caddie Association); I bought a caddie yardage book for six pounds; we spent about fifty pounds on breakfasts, lunches, oranges, and bottled water; we spent about eight pounds over the course of the week buying a two-day-old copy of the *International Herald Tribune* each morning; and Christine spent about thirty pounds gaining admission to various museums and fortresses. When I was finished with the arithmetic, I had arrived at something thrilling: without leading a life of penury, we were able to live off golf. I felt as if I had achieved, at least for a week, a goal: I was a professional amateur.

The caddies working for the Swedes (I learned during a caddie-bus conversation with a looper called Squirrel, who was employed by a Swede) were too well-paid to be considered professional amateurs. The Swedes, one old-timer told me despairingly, were turning caddying into a profession. If you caddied for a Swede you had a real job, and you worked long hours. You'd be on the practice tee through dusk. The seventeen Swedish players on the tour were not like the hundred and fifty or so other touring nomads. Whereas most of the English, Welsh, Scottish, Irish, Spanish, German, Italian, and Argentine players on the tour had grown up in modest financial circumstances, and while most of the Americans, Australians, Canadians, Frenchmen, South Africans, Danes, and New Zealanders on the tour came from something approximating middle-class circumstances, the Swedes, for the most part, were not only born to wealth but also nearly without exception had corporate backers with deep pockets. The Swedish players stayed in plush hotels, ate in good restaurants, wore Ralph Lauren clothes, wintered in Florida or Spain or Monte Carlo, and often traveled with their teachers, psychologists, and fitness advisers, and never on the caddie bus. They spent hours and hours practicing (which isn't a given on the European tour, as it is on the U. S. tour) and listened to inspirational tapes on Sony Walkmans on their way back to the hotel. They didn't play the bouncy, hooking, low-flying British-style game. They hit the ball long and high and straight. They revered technique. They played American golf. (Teravainen, you may have gathered, did not.)

In one way, though, their golf was not American: they did not see the game as fundamentally solitary, as most Americans do. The Swedish players viewed themselves collectively: most of them wore the same hat, with these words stenciled across the front: "Hello, Sweden. Professional Golf Team." They saw their caddie not as an ancillary employee but as an indispensable partner. They had the money to pay whatever was necessary to recruit a top caddie and keep him. Their scale went from two hundred and seventy-five pounds per week to over four hundred pounds. Their bonuses started at five percent for a routine finish to seven and a half percent for a top-ten finish to ten percent for a win. And they did not deduct taxes before figuring the percentage. They wanted good caddies without flamboyant personalities. Anders Forsbrand, who had won only one tournament from his rookie season on the tour in 1982 through 1990, had lured one of the best caddies in all of golf onto his bag: a diminutive curly haired Englishman named Andy Prodger, who had caddied for Faldo when Faldo won his first Masters and his first British Open. Faldo fired Prodger for cryptic reasons. The sacking only enhanced Prodger's standing (Faldo is not liked); the caddie had his pick of bags. Money, no doubt, played a role in Forsbrand's recruitment of Prodger. But Prodger incurred no resentment from his colleagues. He had become a caddie because he wanted to be around the game and wasn't going far as a player himself. His roots were in professional amateurism. I remember in the mid-1980s, when Prodger was working in the United States; his trousers were often tattered and he hung out in the shadows of the clubhouse, seeing everything. Now he was famous. You couldn't regard him as a professional amateur anymore.

I wondered if Teravainen was a professional amateur. As Christine, Peter, and I sat at a plastic table in a roadside cafeteria eating unidentifiable food, somewhere between Tarragona and Madrid, with his pregnant wife thousands of miles away to the east and his parents and siblings thousands of miles away to the west, it occurred to me that there had to be an easier way for Peter to earn a living. He was, after all, a Yale graduate with an astute mind, a degree in Economics, and a skill in a game that remained, a generation after Eisenhower, tremendously useful in the world of commerce.

"I'm doing exactly what I want to be doing," Peter said. "I'm making a living playing golf." He bit into something, and then continued:

"A couple of years ago, I lipped out on a hole where they were offering a million pounds for a hole-in-one, half a million for the player, half a million for charity. I hit a nearly perfect 5-iron shot: bounced once ten feet in front of the hole, then hit inside the cup. When I went up to the hole, I could see the ball mark against the lip. The ball finished a foot from the hole. It was the loudest, quickest gallery burst I've ever heard. For a second there, I figured I had holed it. I thought, 'A half a million pounds—what am I going to do with it?' My heart stopped. Since then, I've thought about it a lot. What would I have done if I had aced that hole, if I had made a half a million pounds, if I didn't need to play the tour anymore to make a living? And the answer I always come up with is that I'd do exactly what I am doing. Maybe I wouldn't ride the caddie bus. Maybe I'd get health insurance. Maybe I'd play a few more tournaments in Asia and a few less in Europe. But basically I'd be doing the same thing. I'd still have the same need to compete.

"That's the thing that worries me: what I'll do when I can no longer compete, when I can't play well enough to make a living out here. I know I'm losing some parts of my game now. I can't hit long irons as long and straight as I once could. It's frightening to see your skills erode. So far, what I've lost in one area I've made up for in another. But that won't always be the case. I wonder what role golf will play in my life when I lose my game. I've got too much respect for the game to play it poorly. I'd like to think that I'd have the strength to give it up—just retire, quit. I know that's hard to do. The respect you have for the game makes you want to stay away from it. The love you have for it brings you back."

A caddie came and told us that the bus was boarding and before too long we were Portugal-bound again. I was starting to think of the caddie bus as the ideal way to travel. As midnight and Madrid approached, I rescinded those thoughts. Something strange had happened; the caddie bus had somehow taken on a life of its own. It became captainless, without a leader, without a direction. Sixty miles outside of Madrid, with no plans to get closer, a movement began, first taking hold in the back of the bus: a paramilitary group was trying to commandeer the bus and head it to a certain disco in Madrid. Turnberry George's assistant, Joey, said, resolutely, the bus was not going to the disco. But since he spoke only English and the bus drivers spoke only Spanish, Joey was at the mercy of two Spanish caddies who were riding free, with seats at the head of the bus, because of their bilingual skills. The services of one of the caddies, named George, had been enlisted by the Madrid Disco Movement. George told the chain-smoking drivers that there had been a change in plan and that the bus would be going into downtown Madrid. Christine briefly joined that Movement, which did not make for matrimonial harmony. Teravainen began shaking his head, but said nothing. He knew trouble was coming. The other bilingual caddie, a stout, silver-bearded man named Dominick, but called King Juan Carlos by the Movement people, simultaneously told the drivers, in a voice louder than George's, that there had *not* been a change in plan.

Meanwhile, another group of caddies, neutral in this dispute, demanded that the music on the bus be made louder. "It's already deafening," Joey shouted back. For the better part of half an hour, anarchy ensued. Things settled down only when Joey announced that the movie would be shown. This was a clever attempt to appease the people, but it backfired. When the opening credits revealed the movie to be *Herbie Rides Again* about a magical VW Bug, the voice of revolt was in the air. When the movie's characters started speaking in Spanish, orange peels, apple cores, and chewing gum wrappers were in the air, too. I hunkered down low in my seat; so did Christine and Peter. She apologized for her earlier position. A game of tackle soccer broke out, with a crushed beer can serving as a ball and the aisle serving as a playing field. I think the head of some red-haired kid was one of the goals. For a while there, it was scary.

In time, people wore themselves out and peace, of an exhausted sort, was restored. By one A.M., there was no noise in the bus at all except snoring, the Spanish mutterings of the two drivers, and the rolling of empty beer bottles up and down the aisle as the caddie bus twisted and turned along the mountainous back roads of Spain, heading for the Portuguese border.

We reached the border gate at half past four and when we did, the bus came to an abrupt stop. It did not take long for the passengers to sense that we were no longer moving, and Joey soon found himself answering pointed questions from the back of the bus.

"What's the holdup?"

"The border's closed."

"When's it open?"

"At six."

"When's the store open?"

"At five."

"They sell beer?"

"Don't know."

"They sell beer?"

"Don't know!"

"They sell beer?"

"Shut up."

"You shut up."

"No, you shut up."

Anarchy resumed.

Five A.M. came and went, but the store did not open. Six A.M. came and went, but the border did not open. Seven A.M. came and went and there was no activity in either the store or the border gate. We were hungry, thirsty, tired, blurry-eyed, and we didn't smell very good. The smell of stale smoke, spilled beer, and unventilated sweat hovered over our heads as we sank lower and lower in our seats, seeking unsuccessfully to find sleeping positions. Our backs ached. At eight A.M., the store finally opened, and it immediately did a brisk business in coffee, beer, and cookies. At eight forty-five a bus load of middle-aged German tourists pulled up behind us, looking perky and crisp. At nine A.M.—earlier predicted as the time we would arrive in Oporto —the border opened. We had been sitting there for more than four hours. At two P.M. we arrived in Oporto and Joey went into a bank. We sat and waited, prisoners of the caddie bus. Three P.M. came and went. I was becoming highly agitated, and a little claustrophobic. Peter, somehow, remained calm. He just sat there silently and read his book. At half past three, Joey returned to the bus and announced that the tournament was not in Oporto but in Povoa de Varzim, a resort town on the Atlantic Ocean an hour north of Oporto. It took two hours to get there.

The bus went first to the official players' hotel where Peter, uncharacteristically, was staying, cutting costs by sharing a room with Willie Aitchison, a veteran caddie who had won three British Opens, twice with Lee Trevino and once with Roberto de Vicenzo. Christine and I got off there, too, hoping to find lodging in the neighborhood. As we retrieved our bags from the belly of the bus, Peter said, "The caddie bus is a lesson in patience, huh?" I took his golf bag to the hotel lobby. "See you tomorrow at eight," he said. At that moment, I would have been hard-pressed to come up with the name of the following day—Monday? Tuesday? Wednesday?—but I knew where I'd be at the appointed time: on the first tee of the Campo de Golf da Estela, venue for the Thirty-fifth Annual Portuguese Open.

After that grueling day-long bus ride, I very much wanted Peter to play well. I felt he deserved to. In the early going, the week unfolded wonderfully. Christine had found elegant lodging at the Grande Hotel, where we had an affordable ocean-front room, owing to early-morning renovation work being done in the lobby. The Portuguese food was delicious. Povoa de Varzim had two movie houses, and the movies were in English. And through thirty-two holes, Peter was only three shots off the lead. Making the cut wasn't even an issue. We were talking leader board! In numbing cold, driving rain, and howling wind (Peter's Ping umbrella didn't survive it), wearing mittens between shots, on a demanding, excellent golf course that was within earshot of the roaring Atlantic surf, Peter was playing magnificently.

Then on the thirty-third hole, disaster struck. The hole was a short, straightforward downwind par-four of 413 yards—a birdie hole. With the fairway firm and running, players who hit drivers left themselves with pitch shots into the green. But there was an out-of-bounds far off the left side of the fairway and since accuracy mattered off the tee more than length, Peter decided to play safe. He hit a 2-iron and he smothered it, a duck hook. The ball would have exited the golf-course property completely (which would have resulted in a two-shot penalty), but a two-foot-high cement retaining wall kept it in play. From almost against the wall, his only shot was backwards. He chopped down with a sand wedge and pitched the ball onto the fairway, and had 235 yards to the hole for his third.

Unfortunately, the resulting shot called for the 2-iron, a club now riddled in disrepute. Guarding against the hook, Peter pushed this 2-iron shot, hitting his ball to the right of a greenside bunker and onto a hard dirt path. With a sand wedge again, he caught the ball off the flange and it flew over the green, down a hill, and into a huge patch of sopping wet yard-high grass. Three caddies, three players, and two spectators began a comprehensive hands-and-knees search for a missing balata-covered, 100-compression Titleist 384 stamped with the numeral 8. The rules allow five minutes to search for a lost ball. If you fail to find it, you go back to the spot where you played your last shot and incur a two-stroke penalty. I began searching for the ball frantically, realizing that if the ball wasn't found, we might well miss the cut. The leader board was fast becoming a memory.

With about fifteen seconds remaining on the five minutes, one of the caddies unearthed the ball, snarled in thick, wet grass. Peter took a huge, slashing swing at it, with a sand wedge, and it went flying over the green into a bunker, where it finished in an awkward little depression. In playing out of that bunker Teravainen's ball skittered across the green to another bunker. He made a good shot from there and holed a three-foot putt for a quadruple-bogey eight. Suddenly, he needed to play good golf over the remaining three holes just to qualify for weekend play.

Not many players would have stayed calm during the making of that eight, and certainly not after it. But Peter—who is perfectly capable of, as old-time golf people say, "losing the head"—kept cool, kept his head right on. He hadn't played the thirty-third hole so very poorly: all he did was make one bad shot, which led to a series of bad shots. I believe that the interminable caddie bus trip, which Peter took as a "lesson in patience," helped Peter accept his fate on the thirty-third with equanimity. After the disaster, he did what he had to do to make the cut. He was shaky, nervous, and upset. He played the final three holes very cautiously; you could see how restricted his swing had become. But he made a birdie and two pars coming in, and made the cut by two shots. On the weekend, his good play returned, and he finished the tournament in a tie for thirteenth and made £4,052. He was quite pleased with that. I kept thinking that it could have been so much better. He kept thinking that he wouldn't have made a single pound had that caddie not found his ball.

During the week of the Portuguese Open there was discussion of organizing an "elite" caddie bus for the very long trip to Italy, for the Florence Open. Teravainen warned me not to be impressed by the word "elite," which he said was used as part of a crass marketing ploy on the part of the bus organizers. "There's always the promise of selectivity," Peter told me. "It never happens." Peter decided to fly to Florence from Oporto, by way of London. Christine and I decided to go by train. Five trains and fifty-six hours later, we were there.

The Ugolino Golf Club, site of the Florence Open and just outside the city, was an old, stylish, and lovely course, dismissed by the players, who were put off by the sluggish greens and a length that was short even by country-club standards, let alone the unearthly standards of the modern tournament professional. It was a par-72 of just 6,280 yards, with three or four drivable par-fours and par-fives that could all be reached with middle-iron second shots. If you didn't break 70 every day there, you weren't in the running. The winner was Anders Forsbrand, the Swede, with Andy Prodger, Faldo's former caddie, on his bag.

Peter was not in the running, not even for the cut. I suppose a letdown was inevitable. We had made four straight cuts together, including two top-fifteen finishes. We were working well together. In Florence, I believe, Peter's thoughts were to the east. After Florence, he was returning to Singapore for two weeks to see his wife (the tour had an off week followed by a tournament on the island of Jersey, which Peter was skipping). In the back of his mind, I suspect, was the idea that a missed cut meant a two-day head start in getting home. I was not surprised at all when he failed to qualify for the final two rounds. Several times in Portugal he mentioned how much he disliked Italy and the Ugolino golf course. At one point in the first round at Ugolino he said, "Why do I bother coming to this place?" No answer was forthcoming.

After Florence, Christine and I went to the island of Malta, and stayed there during the off week. We were lured to Malta by the promise of weather warmer than Greece, with golf left from its days as a British colony. Though the temperature never even approached seventy degrees, and the Royal Malta Golf Club turned out to be a field with holes, we had a wonderful week away from the singular world of the European golf tour. We stayed in a sixteenth-century palace in the ancient walled city of Mdina, a beautiful place. The caddie bus, the long trip to Florence, and Peter's play there seemed very far behind us. We stayed on in Malta during the week of the Jersey Open, and then flew to London.

By Sunday, April 14, we had made our way to Cornwall, in southern England. This was the day before I was to meet Peter for the start of practice for the Benson & Hedges International. It was also the day of the final round of the Masters. In looking for a bed-and-breakfast in Cornwall, I regarded a working television as the chief requirement.

On the closing holes of the last round of the 1991 Masters, three players were in position to win: Ian Woosnam, José-María Olazábal, and Tom Watson. Each of them had something to prove: Woosnam that he had the desire to win a major title, Olazábal that he had the golfing maturity to win a major, and Watson that he had his psychic and golfing house in order. Just a few months earlier, Watson had resigned his membership at the Kansas City Country Club, where his family has belonged for generations. The club had rejected for membership a well-regarded and prominent local man, Henry Bloch, a founder of the H & R Block tax-preparation company, solely, Watson believed, because of Bloch's religion. Bloch is Jewish. Watson is not Jewish, but his wife and children are. He quit, and even when the club subsequently invited Bloch to join, Watson did not return.

I had admired Watson, a five-time British Open champion, before his resignation from the Kansas City Country Club, and admired him more afterwards. He was my favorite American golfer, and I was rooting for him at Augusta. Until the thirteenth. That was when, even on TV, you could hear cheering and see arm-raising when Woosnam, playing with Watson in the day's final pairing, drove his ball into Rae's Creek. The American spectators were for the American, and that, I suppose, was to be expected. But to cheer against a player is not the way of golf. They were jingoistic cheers, and they embarrassed me. When an announcer reminded us that Watson had twice before won the

Masters, I decided that he didn't need the win as much as Woosnam now deserved it, and I changed my allegiance in mid-course.

If you saw it, you probably recall the tournament's denouement at the eighteenth, the uphill well-bunkered par-four that curves to the right. Olazábal came to the final tee at eleven under par in a three-way tie for the lead with Watson and Woosnam. Off that last tee, Olazábal, playing in the penultimate pairing of the day, drove into a bunker on the left side of the fairway. His second shot came to rest in a greenside bunker. His bunker shot stopped forty feet short of the hole and his first putt left him with a three-footer for bogey, which he made. For him to stay alive, he needed the last two men on the course to make bogeys or worse.

Watson, teeing off first, tried to increase his chances of finding the narrow fairway by hitting a 3-wood shot off the tee. But he pushed the shot directly into a grove of sturdy trees from which he would have done well to make bogey. He didn't. His six left him a shot behind Olazábal.

Woosnam hit a driver off the final tee and smashed it; the ball flew 275 yards, carrying over the bunker that Olazábal had found. His approach shot left him twenty paces from the hole. He played his third shot with a putter, even though he was a yard off the green, and the ball rolled six feet past the hole. If he missed the par putt, there would be a playoff between the two Europeans. He holed it.

Ever since Ballesteros became the first European to win at Augusta in 1980, Europeans have been dominating the Masters. Ballesteros won again in 1983. Bernhard Langer won in 1985. Sandy Lyle won in 1988. Nick Faldo won in 1989 and 1990. And now Woosnam had won in 1991, with Olazábal right behind him. Straight from Augusta, Woosnam would be coming to Cornwall. He would be returning to his tour as conquering hero.

CHAPTER SIX

Woosie

EVEN BY THE MODEST STANDARDS of professional amateurism, our family finances hit a low ebb in late April. We turned a modest profit in Portugal, spent the booty in Florence, went into deficit spending in the two following golf-free weeks, broke even at the Benson & Hedges International (Peter finished in twenty-fourth place and earned £4,140), and sustained further losses in the following week, at the Madrid Open (forty-third place, £1,540). With my wallet dangerously emaciated, I called *Golf Digest,* looking for work. They wanted me to write a profile of Ian Woosnam, and that made me happy. But they wanted me to see the new Masters champion in his hometown, Oswestry, in Wales, and that did not. Going to Wales would require me to leave the tour for a week, and I had a sinking feeling that the week I was off the circuit would be the week Peter would win.

I would have been pleased had Peter been somewhat hesitant to grant me a one-week leave of absence. He wasn't. So on the Sunday after the Madrid Open, with the tour heading east for the Côte d'Azur and the Cannes Open, I flew north to Oswestry, courtesy of *Golf Digest,* while Christine ventured off by train to Morocco.

I knew that Oswestry was the center of Woosnam's universe. He had said so before making his exit from the Benson & Hedges, where he shot 82-82. He missed the cut by eight strokes, collected his six-figure appearance fee, and split for a month at home. I saw immediately the town's appeal. Oswestry was a small, prosperous, and handsome market town on the border of England and Wales with a pleasant main street and a cattle auction every Wednesday. It had several good restaurants, a well-stocked bookstore, a movie house, and a good hotel. It was a town that seemed to have changed little in the past thirty or forty years.

Woosnam's homeland—rural and rugged Shropshire County, which was also the boyhood home of Sandy Lyle—was sprawling, but all of life there seemed connected. When I got to Oswestry, Woosnam and his wife, Glendryth, were on the front page of the weekly *Oswestry and Border Counties Advertizer,* in a color picture, with matching smiles, their fingers wrapped identically around blue tea mugs. On a page toward the back, under the heading "Golf returns . . ." there was an item about Mrs. Joan Woosnam, mother of the Masters champion, competing in the Bronze Division of the Ladies' Golf Union Coronation Foursome, taking the medal honor with a net 90. Woosnam's parents lived in a cottage a short walk away from The Wynnstay, the hotel where I was staying. Woosnam's house—red-brick, charming, and modest, given his success—was just a mile away, down the Morda Road, on a leafy property bordered by a cricket club, a sheep meadow, and a little housing development. When I stopped for gas ten miles or so out of town, the attendant showed me where the Woosnams had farmed until just a few years earlier. The first golf course I passed was the Oswestry Golf Club, where Mrs. Woosnam had carded her net 90 in the Coronation Foursome. The second one I saw, the Llanymynech Golf Club, was the one where Woosnam had done most of his playing as a boy. A third one, the Hill Valley Golf Club, was where Woosnam had lived in a converted cow shed in his teens, and where he had worked with a man who later became the manager of The Wynnstay, who was organizing a Masters victory party for Woosnam. Everything seemed tidy, nice, and calm.

Ian's telephone number was not listed, but the number for his father, Harold, was. I called him up and he invited me over.

"What kind of story is it that you're going to write?" he asked.

When I heard that question I knew I was back to reporting. Reporters hear that question routinely. I think the question is often a code for, "Are you going to do a hatchet job?"

"I'd like to write a profile of Ian, write a story about what he's like."

"Yes?" Harold Woosnam said. He wanted more.

"I'd like to find out how he became the player he is, and why he won his first major when he did." Woosnam has been one of the leading players in the game since 1982, and some people were surprised that it took him so long to win a major.

"Well, that all sounds fine, but you'll not get Ian for at least a couple days—they've got him all tied up with these corporate outings," Harold said. It was a Monday night, just past dinner, and he was wearing plaid slippers. His *they* referred to agents at IMG, the International Management Group, which represents Woosnam's business interests. In the modern era of big-time sports, which golf has only recently joined, nearly anything that is unpopular about an athlete—that he charges for his autograph; that he boycotts practice sessions over contractual disputes; that he is unresponsive to his public, which pays him; that he is inaccessible to the public's representative, the press—is blamed on the agent. While it is true that the agents are often greedy, shortsighted, and obnoxious, they do not work in a vacuum. They are empowered by their client, who is the boss. The agent, like the caddie, is an employee. So it wasn't entirely fair of Harold Woosnam to blame the agents for his son's hectic schedule.

"I've got all week," I said.

"I don't know that he's talking to any of you guys," Harold Woosnam said. He was a sturdy-looking man, about three inches taller than Ian (who is five-four and a half), with thick hair combed straight back, skin lined handsomely by the wind and the sun, and a hacking cough. He smoked cigarillos.

"Why not? He's the Masters champion," I said.

"Yes, but you're costing him time, and you're not paying him," Harold Woosnam said. Behind him, on a wall, were the trophies of his farming career. In 1972, Harold was awarded a blue ribbon for a Northwestern British Friesian Breeder at the Crewe Fair, a major British agricultural festival. Soon afterwards, he moved from livestock to cereal. Less profitable, but more predictable, the switch allowed Harold to attend Ian's junior tournaments, where he often caddied for his son. I could only imagine how much golf must have meant to them then, how dominating it must have been in their conversation. That was twenty years ago. Now, I was a nuisance because I wanted to talk golf without paying for it. *You're costing him time, and you're not paying him.*

"Is that what it's come to?" I asked.

Harold Woosnam dragged on his cigarillo and squinted his eyes until you couldn't see them at all. His years of smoking had rendered his voice deep and throaty; he was a bass with the North Wales Voice Association. "Thing is, it wasn't that long ago that he was dying for attention. Now he's got more than he needs. If you weren't from America, I would've told you to bugger off. But there are millions to be made in America."

Right then, I wished I had never called *Golf Digest.* I wished that I was in Cannes, carrying Teravainen's bag. We sat in silence. I thumbed through an old scrapbook, crowded with scores of pictures, letters, and newspaper clippings about Ian, cut with pride and care but now starting to yellow. One story, from *The Daily Telegraph,* about the 1975 British Boys Championship, concluded with this: "[Brian] Marchbank takes on Ian Woosnam, of Wales, a sturdy, beautifully balanced little fighter with a lovely swing and plenty of power. Wales have unearthed a really good player here." Can you imagine how excited the Woosnams must have been when they read *that* in a big London newspaper? A page or so later there was a hand-written note, on Welsh Golfing Union stationery, congratulating an eighteen-year-old Ian on his selection to the 1976 Welsh National team. The note, from the union's secretary, said, "I will send you a Welsh players' tie and a Welsh badge, which please have sewn to a dark blue blazer."

This was in a period when Ian was scrounging for sweaters in lost-and-found boxes. Can you imagine the tingly scurrying that must have gone on in the Woosnam house around then, when they went to the closet to inspect the quality, fit, and shade of Ian's old blazer? *Harold, do you think we can afford a new one? Oh, I reckon so, Joan.* My thoughts drifted to my early years in golf—in that same period, the mid-1970s—when I became hopelessly infatuated with the game, and my mother lovingly sewed little golf-bag emblems to my summer shirts and looked for clubs at yard sales and in the basement of the Salvation Army. I looked at Harold Woosnam. He was watching television. For a moment, my little golfing adventure seemed pointless. The game was no different abroad; it had spiraled out of control the world over. I was feeling melancholy. My wife, now my wife of six months, was in Marrakesh or Meknes or Rabat, I did not know where. I only knew that I had no way to reach her. My parents were far away, and so were my friends, in golf and out of golf. I missed my newspaper, and Philadelphia, and my home golf course. I was sick of following baseball through the abbreviated box scores of the *International Herald Tribune.* I was tired of living out of a bag. My subject seemed hopelessly selfish.

Harold Woosnam suggested I write a note to Ian, explaining my purpose and asking him to call me at his convenience, and put it in his mailbox. "Tell him you're a caddie, I don't think he'd turn down a caddie," Harold said. I did just as he suggested, and put the note in his mailbox that night, and went to sleep.

After that first Monday evening at Harold Woosnam's cottage, I limited my wanderings from The Wynnstay. I figured that Ian Woosnam could possibly call at any moment and that he might want me to come straight over, and I didn't want to risk missing that. Occasionally, I would go out, interview somebody, and hurry back. I realize now that I made myself a prisoner of the hotel.

On Tuesday morning, I drove to the Oswestry Golf Club, regarded as the rich man's club of Shropshire, but a simple and unpretentious place nonetheless, where I met a man named Pip Speake, a friend of Harold Woosnam's and a farm products salesman. He told a story about Ian and himself as golf partners.

"We were playing together in an interclub match, twenty years ago. A boiling hot day it was, everybody red-faced and sweating. I took a cold drink out of my bag, gave Ian a sip, took one for myself. 'We better give our opponents a sip, they'll die of thirst,' I said. Ian grabs the container, shoves it in his bag, and says, 'To hell with that.' " Pip Speake shook his head at the memory.

I returned to the hotel hoping to find a message. There wasn't one.

On Wednesday morning, I spoke with Peter Condliffe, the manager of The Wynnstay, who had worked with Ian in the 1970s at the Hill Valley Golf Club. In 1977, Woosnam had decided that he wanted to try the tour, but he had no money. Condliffe organized a party for Woosnam which raised £350, enough to launch the voyage. Fourteen years later, Condliffe was organizing a Masters victory party for two hundred, for which Woosnam was paying. Condliffe was recreating the thirteenth hole at Augusta, complete with bunkers made of rice and a miniature Rae's Creek flowing with champagne cocktail.

I spent the rest of the day reading, writing letters, and waiting for the phone to ring. The Masters champ never called.

On Thursday afternoon, I talked to Col. Arthur Jones, one of the old hands of Welsh golf, who had presided over the 1971 Shropshire and Hereford Counties Junior Championship. "My practice in those days was to write a little post-match speech for the winner and the runner-up so that they could get in the habit of saying thank you," the colonel said. The 1971 junior championship was won by Sandy Lyle, older than Woosnam by three weeks. "I gave Sandy the winner's speech and I gave Woosie the consolation speech. Woosie shoved his speech in his back pocket and said, 'I'll beat you one day, Sandy Lyle.' "

That evening, I was in my room, watching a BBC show about auto-theft prevention, when the telephone rang. I jumped out of bed.

"Have you heard from Ian yet?" Harold Woosnam wanted

to know. "Well, maybe you will and maybe you won't. I've put in a good word for you and that's all I can do." I thanked him for that, but I was losing hope.

On Friday afternoon, I drove over to see Alex Lyle, Sandy's Scottish-born father, and the retired club professional of the Hawkstone Park Hotel golf course, twenty miles from Oswestry. I asked Alex Lyle about the youthful competition between Ian and Sandy. "Ian saw it as a great rivalry, but Sandy did not," he said. "Even at a young age, Sandy understood the idea of playing the golf course, playing yourself. Ian's attitude was, 'I'm going to beat this bloke.' "

When I returned to the hotel, a bartender said, "You just missed Ian." I asked if he had, by any chance, asked for me. "No, don't think so," the barman said. "He came to check on the party arrangements. No queries for you, so far as I know."

Saturday afternoon I went by Joan and Harold Woosnam's, to return a scrapbook I had borrowed from them. "Did you get your story?" Harold asked me. Not really, I said. "All you wanted was an interview with Ian?" Harold asked. Pretty much, I said. "All right," Harold said, "I'll tell you about Ian."

And he did. He sat down in his favorite chair, put his cigarillos on a side table, and spelled it all out for me: how Ian Woosnam came to be the golfer he is, and why he won his first major when he did, according to his father.

"Ian's a lot like me," Harold Woosnam said. "I'm not saying he's not his own man, because he is. He's thirty-three, and he's very much his own man. But he's a battler, and so am I. When I was a boy, I wanted to be a boxer. I would rather have boxed than ate breakfast. I could have been very good. I even went as far as to get a manager. But my parents squashed it. They said, 'You can farm, or you can get out.' The day I turned fourteen, I brought a note to my schoolteacher from my mother. It said, 'Needed to work on farm.' That was my last day of school.

"Later, I wanted to be a footballer. I was on the county team.

For two years there, the game looked positively easy to me. I was too good for my class. I should have tried the professional ranks. I would have been very good, but I got no encouragement from my father.

"In the fifties, I found myself needing a sport. I couldn't box and I couldn't play football. In those days, hardly anybody around here played golf. They played in Scotland, and in England, but farmers here didn't have the time, the interest, or the money for it. One day, four top players—let's see if I can remember them: Max Faulkner, Ken Bousfield, Harry Weetman, and Neil Coles—came to Oswestry for an exhibition. I went, I tried the game, and I liked it straight off, even though I kept missing the ball. I could see the challenge. It suited me down to the ground.

"When Joan and I got married, I vowed that I wouldn't do as my parents had done. I'd encourage the children into sports, support them as best I could. Ian started boxing at age five, and he was good at it. Too good. His opponents always ended up with bloody noses. So nobody would box him. He started swimming. On his own. And he became good at it. At seven, he took up football and golf. He *excelled* at them. He was determined to be a professional sportsman in something. It didn't particularly matter what. He wanted it. I encouraged him, but I never pushed him. His desire came from within. If I had ever told him, 'You can farm, or you can get out,' I think he would have left.

"His shortness affected him profoundly. Some people say it didn't, but I know it did. He always wanted to show that he was as good as the big man. He became as strong as anybody, as strong as big Sandy Lyle. You know how Ian's arms got so big? By driving a tractor as a boy, that's how. He never had it easy. You know how far it was from our farm to the nearest golf course? Fourteen miles. Sandy Lyle had the golf course right outside his house. He had all the equipment. Even as a boy, he had professional caddies. His father was a professional teacher. Ian didn't have any of that. I played off five, I could show him a few things, but it's not the same as real tuition. He had to scrounge for equipment. I had to caddie for him. He was so wild, but long! Ian welcomed the obstacles. The headmaster of his school told him to go to the agricultural college. He said professional golf was too financially—what word did he use?—insecure. We talked about it. A farmer in those days might earn five thousand pounds in a top year. I told Ian if he thought he could make two or three thousand pounds a year playing professional golf, enough to make a living, then he should do it. He'd be his own boss. That was one of the biggest things: nobody would tell him what to do, he'd do what he wanted. His goal was to make a living at it. I never envisioned anything beyond that. At first, I don't think he did, either.

"He always associated professional golf with money. We grew up on a farm. We weren't poor, but we didn't have any money. Money mattered, mattered a great deal to us. The guy he admired most was the guy who won the most money. He figured that the man who made the most money was the best player. When he finished first on the Order of Merit, in 1987, he won over four hundred thousand pounds, and he thought he had really made it. Then last year, he won the Order of Merit again, and this time it was over seven hundred thousand pounds, but it wasn't as satisfying. He saw what Faldo had done, winning the Open championship and the Masters in the same year. He saw that people attached more value to that, financially, and in terms of prestige. I think it made him think about the majors in a different way. He certainly didn't grow up hearing about the majors. Three of them are American anyhow, right? I can't say that I can even name the four majors. But he caught on as to the value of them. He got it in his head that he had to win a major. And that's the way he is. He gets these ideas in his head, and then he makes them happen: I'm going to make a living playing golf; I'm going to finish first on the Order of Merit; I'm going to win a major.

"The way that Masters unfolded, with Ian and Tom Watson playing in the final group, tied for the lead most of the day, that was ideal for Ian. One man against the other. I didn't know how he'd respond to Watson, though. In the late seventies, when Ian was starting out as a pro, he idolized Watson. He talked about him all the time, Watson this and Watson that. One day I pulled him aside. I said, 'This Tom Watson, does he have anything you don't have? Does he have three arms?' I never heard much about Tom Watson after that. But as they were playing, I didn't know what kind of feelings Ian still had for him. I thought he might be intimidated by him.

"After Ian won, I was probably as happy as he was. I probably wanted it for him nearly as much as he wanted it for himself. But I would never have had the courage to make that last putt. In my dreams, I see myself standing over it, but I can't bring the putter head back. Those six feet to win look like six miles.

"People are always making fun of me because I don't believe in giving putts. At the club, if there's a dispute over whether a putt should be given they say, 'Would Harold give it?' The answer is always, 'No.' The thing is, that's when the game starts to get really interesting, when you *have* to make putts. That's when you start playing the game only in your head. The putt he made to win, to me, it was frightening. I was sitting right here in this room, and I could barely watch. Ian welcomed it. That's the difference between us.

"I wasn't surprised that he made it. I wasn't surprised that he won. I figured if he could get himself into position to win, he'd win. The thing that did surprise me was to see Watson push that last tee shot into the trees. With all his experience, you'd think he'd have been able to make the swing he needed to make there. But he didn't. It just goes to show you how fleeting it all is. One day you have it, one day you don't. All of a sudden it's gone, *pffffff,* and nobody knows where it went. So you make it while you can."

When Harold Woosnam was finished, I sat in his den, dumbfounded. Suddenly, I saw Ian in a completely different light. I understood that Ian Woosnam followed in the tradition of Byron Nelson, who saw each tournament paycheck as a step closer to making the farm of his dreams—and retirement from the wrenching life of tournament golf—a reality. Whatever hostility I had felt toward my subject earlier now seemed misplaced. Later that day I bumped into Ian in the parking lot of the Oswestry Golf Club. He was friendly. He said he just didn't feel like giving interviews, he didn't feel like talking about the Masters, he didn't feel like talking about golf. "I'm just trying to get away," he said. I said I understood. Would I be at the Italian Open, he asked. Yes, I said. I'll give you whatever you need there, he said.

On Monday morning, I checked out of The Wynnstay, preparing to return to the tour. While eating breakfast, I checked the papers to see how Peter had fared at Cannes—I wanted him to play well, but not so well that he would think that he could play better without me. He opened with 71, 73, to make the cut on the number, and finished 73, 69 for joint eighteenth place. Who had been on his bag? I wondered. The hotel was starting to fill up with Woosnam's friends, coming in for the victory party to be held that night. Sam Torrance came in. So did Phil Morbey, Woosnam's caddie. And Bob Torrance and his wife. Cases of champagne were brought in, to fill the re-creation of Rae's Creek. I made a note about the bunker made of rice, and felt the pull of my adopted profession.

CHAPTER SEVEN

WINDFALLS

OVER THE NEXT TEN WEEKS—at the Spanish Open, the Italian Open, the European P. G. A. Championship, the British Masters, the Murphy's Cup, the Belgian Open, the Irish Open, the French Open, the Monte Carlo Open, and the Scottish Open—Christine and I became addicted to our new lives. Which is not to say they were an unending pleasure. Often the weather was horrible; in Ireland, in late June, we were cold, wet, and windblown for a week. More than once we had things stolen; in Madrid, a car we had rented was broken into and ten rolls of exposed film and a pair of golf shoes belonging to Peter were taken. Some of the journeys were interminable; Monte Carlo to Scotland took parts of three days and an overnight ferry. Sometimes the food was inedible; we drove one two-hundred-mile stretch in Spain where the only places to eat were trash-strewn tapas bars choking with cigarette smoke and swarming with flies, drunken men, and hookers. At times we traveled sick; I have a picture of my wife and me standing in three feet of snow in mid-May in the Andorran Pyrenees, the lone time she, inveterate traveler, was vertical during a two-day Madrid-to-Milan drive. Occasionally the search for cheap digs, as Teravainen called them, wore us out; after three frazzling hours scouting the northern Italian resort towns along Lago Maggiore, we found the last available bed. But it turned out to be a good bed, at a fair price, above a nice restaurant owned by a friendly family, in a comfortable room with hot and cold water. Early morning, when we stuck our heads outside the bedroom window, we saw our reflections in the still lake below us, and across the lake we saw the Swiss Alps, glimmering.

Our lives had been turned over to serendipity. On an Ireland-to-France ferry crossing, for which we had no reservation (we *never* made reservations), we were the last car aboard the day's last ferry. On the Monte Carlo-to-Scotland drive, we stopped at a small and unassuming open-air restaurant on the French Riviera called L'Oasis, perched between a busy coastal road and a steep cliff, with a view of the Mediterranean, and had there the best lunch of our trip. All it was was good roasted chicken, its deliciousness bound in its unexpectedness.

Beyond the itinerary of the tour, which gave our lives structure, we had no plan, for anything. When we were in Waterloo for the Belgian Open, we rented a room in a private house and, as it turned out (indispensable phrase!), the woman who owned the house owned an apartment in Paris, too. So, two weeks later, when we went to Paris for the French Open, we rented it, a tiny, wonderful flat in Montmartre. We managed to stretch our stay there to nine nights. Christine bought a French cookbook, a case of wine, and cooked brilliantly. We ate out once.

During the week of the French Open, Christine suggested that I invite Peter back to the apartment for dinner, but I didn't think that was something he'd want to do. In four months, we had eaten only two dinners together, and neither of those had been planned. The first time was when the Spain-to-Portugal caddie bus made a roadside stop. The second time was even less deliberate. Christine and I had just sat down for dinner at an Indian restaurant in Woburn, during the week of the British Masters, when Peter and his wife walked in. We waved them over and they joined us (Veronica, then about midway through her pregnancy, traveled with Peter for one three-week stint). Dinner was very pleasant, but all through it I could not help but think of Peter's substantial burden: his golfing skill was supporting all four of us, and a fifth on the way. And then he insisted on paying for dinner.

Anyway (as I tried to explain to Christine), professional golfers in competition don't like to commit themselves to social engagements, because that means committing to a social mood, and that is a difficult thing for the professional golfer to do. Since golf offers little opportunity for the physical release of stress, the feelings of anger and worthlessness after a bad round—say a 78 with thirty-eight putts and a ball out of bounds on the last—can linger well into the night. Given the suffocating internality of tournament golf, it is surprising to me that the professional game does not routinely produce examples of mentally unstable behavior.

Not that you don't see some weird things from time to time. In the second round of the Spanish Open, Peter was paired with a player named Armando Saavedra, a veteran player from Argentina. Saavedra, a good golfer who has never played to his ability and who has struggled annually to keep his tour privileges, was playing nicely through thirty-four holes, just a couple of shots off the lead. Then on the thirty-fifth hole he missed an eighteen-inch putt for par. *Smack!* As hard as he could he slapped himself across his cheek with an open hand. I could not believe it—he had inflicted real pain on himself. And then, as if nothing out of the ordinary had happened, he calmly handed his putter back to his caddie, who did not dare to make eye contact with him. For just a moment there, tournament golf had taken its toll: Saavedra had lost the head.

Two weeks earlier, at the Madrid Open, Stephen Bennett, normally a mild-mannered and pleasant Englishman, was paired with Peter when Bennett lapsed into temporary insanity. He was attempting a ten-foot par putt as a scorekeeper, a teenaged boy with a walkie-talkie in hand, was relaying results to the press tent. *"Quatro, quatro, cinco."* Bennett tried to get the kid's attention, but wasn't successful. So he putted, and wasn't successful in that effort, either. He marched toward the Spanish boy, got three steps away from him and raised the middle finger of his right hand directly at the kid. The youth responded blankly—

no anger, nothing. This seemed to enrage Bennett even more. He stepped right up to the boy and raised his middle finger again, inches from the kid's face. The boy angled his head and looked quizzically at Bennett, but did not move or speak. I believe he had no understanding of Bennett's gesture, none at all. Bennett stormed off and the kid shrugged. For the rest of the day, and for all of the next, Bennett's play was miserable. In the second round, Bennett charged his caddie with carrying a dry towel (part should always be damp for cleaning), made a ten when he lost two balls on one hole, putted with the outside toe of his putter, and missed the cut easily. He had lost the head.

The incident happened, I have come to realize, because Bennett, like every tournament golfer, has a perfectionist element to his personality. In his mind he would have made that putt had it not been for the kid. You never know what will upset a golfer's fragile balance.

Six weeks after that, at the Belgian Open, a trim, cerebral American player named Ron Stelten came to me and said, "Did you read that load of crap in *The European?*"

"Which load of crap is that?"

"They've got a guy writing about the U. S. Open. He says, 'Since the Roaring Twenties, only two non-Americans have won the U. S. Open, Tony Jacklin and David Graham.' You see anything *wrong* with that sentence?" Stelten's eyes, Midwestern and bright blue, were wild with rage.

"He left out Gary Player." Player, a South African, won at the Bellerive Country Club in St. Louis in 1965, when Stelten was nine.

"That's right—they left out Gary Player. Gary Player! Only one of the greatest golfers of all time. I mean, it really scares you, it really makes you worry. If they can make a mistake like that, what can you trust? Is *anything* accurate? Can you read anything that's *right?*"

It is possible that what was truly bothering Stelten was that the U. S. Open was being played at the Hazeltine Golf Club, in Chaska, Minnesota—a course on which Stelten grew up caddying and which he still regards as a golfing home—while he was unsuccessfully struggling to make the cut at the Belgian Open, and that some guy who omitted Gary Player's name from a list of non-American U. S. Open winners *was* there. But more likely (and I am on loose and dangerous ground here, trying to guess the complex workings of a professional golfer's mind) was that Stelten was simply appalled by the inaccuracy, the inattention to factual detail. Golfers, as a group, crave facts. They deal in accurate information. If Stelten turns in a card that says he took 71 strokes to negotiate a course, then it took him 71 strokes. If he tells you he had 167 yards for his second shot on the fourth, then he had 167 yards. If he tells you the only reason he missed a putt was that he played it two balls outside on the high side and it was, in actual fact, straight, then the putt was, in actual fact, straight, and your theories about why he missed the putt—whether they concern a gust of wind or a wobbly stroke or hard luck or gallery distractions or a pitch mark or God or fate—are wrong. If God or fate kept the ball out of the hole, the golfer will tell you.

The thing I liked best about Teravainen was that he was consumed with factual accuracy. He was truthful. He was so truthful he could actually analyze the losing of the head while it was coming off. At the Florence Open, he told me, "I'm losing it, I'm losing it, I'm fighting it, but I'm losing it," as his golfing troubles mounted during one particular bad patch. On one hole, a short par-four, he used the word *fuck* about fourteen times. This was not like him. At the turn, he inquired about a medical leave from the tournament. He knew he had lost the head and that he could do no good that week.

Facts were his specialty. If Peter told you Dwight Gooden was scheduled to pitch on a Tuesday night and you didn't see Gooden's name in the Thursday box scores in the *International Herald Tribune,* then you knew something had happened to him. If you told Peter that the London papers were running stories saying Greg Norman was planning a return to the European tour and he told you that the chances of that happening were *extremely* remote, then the chances were extremely remote. If you told Peter that he was due on the first tee in three minutes and he told you your watch was a minute fast and he actually had four minutes, then your watch was a minute fast and he actually had four minutes. He was a precise man, an accurate man, and I admired that: he was reliable, and he was also self-reliant. He demanded a great deal of himself, but expected nothing from others. With one exception: his caddie.

In the Rules of Golf, a player's caddie is a legal extension of himself, and I think that is precisely how Teravainen saw me. I believe that in his treatment of me, I had the rare opportunity to see exactly how a person treats himself. He was demanding of me, and he expected a high level of competence from me, but he was seldom harsh, usually fair, and he saw no point in bothering with conventional politeness. Whenever I got angry at him, I would say to myself: I am his caddie and that makes me a legal extension of him; he is treating me as he would treat himself.

For instance, one afternoon in Monte Carlo, I offered him a ride to the golf course for the following morning. We had agreed upon leaving at half past seven. When I returned to my hotel room at about eleven that night, there was a note from Peter: "I want to leave at seven so I can have breakfast at the club." That was it, not even a soupçon of politeness. It was rude.

Christine wrote on the back of the note: "Pete, The car leaves at 7:30. If you need it sooner, bus it.—The Bambergers."

I would have loved to have returned that note to him, but of course I did not. I was a legal extension of Peter, he was not a legal extension of me. At seven A.M. I was outside his hotel.

He was usually fair. At the Florence Open, he sent me up to a blind green. "Tell me if the pin is on the upper shelf or the lower shelf," he said. I climbed the hill to the green, and I saw no shelves at all, just a gentle slope from top to bottom, and the hole was cut in the center of the green. "It's in the middle," I yelled back to him.

I could see Peter shaking his head in the fairway, as he propped himself up on his sand wedge. He made no effort to hide his disgust. "Can't be in the middle. Top shelf or bottom shelf?"

I could think of no answer that would satisfy him. "To me, it looks middle," I said.

Peter hit his shot, not well but on the green. He didn't know how firmly to hit the wedge. He two-putted for his par, and when we came off the green he said, "You're right, the green has no tiers."

Only once did I think Peter was being unfair. That happened at the Italian Open (where Woosnam did give me my interview) and I was so surprised by his lapse that it caused me, momentarily, to fantasize about firing him. I'll tell you about it, but first, some background.

In golf, there are some players who talk to their golf ball, and others who don't. Likewise, there are caddies who talk to their player's golf ball, and caddies who don't. Peter was a talker. If he hit a shot well, and felt he deserved a good result, he'd say, "Be nice, baby, be nice." Sometimes that came out like this: "Be nice, baby, benicebenicebenice." If a drive was sailing toward a bunker, he might yell, "Fly!" If a chip appeared to have too much steam to stop near the hole, he might say, "Settle now, settle, settle, settle. Settle, goddamnit!" If he was in a negative mood and a shot was heading out-of-bounds, he might say, "Go out of bounds, get out." I was a talker, too, although not to that degree, but a definite, moderate talker. I have talked to golf balls all my golfing life. I accept that a golf ball is inanimate; I understand that a golf ball does not have ears or a brain or even a nervous system. But it is, nonetheless, pleasing to see a golf ball pop right out of a bunker at the exact moment you've yelled, "Skip, golf ball, skip!" So, yes, I talk to golf balls; I admit to that. If I had to guess, I'd say we talkers are in the majority.

During the third round of the Italian Open, on the eighth hole, a par-five, Peter hit his second shot over the green and into the woods. He hit a delicate chip out of the woods, a very tricky play, and the ball slid past the hole, just missing the pin. As it passed the hole, the ball showed no signs of weariness. As it approached the short fringe grass between the green and a greenside bunker, I said, "Sit down, golf ball," just once and in a low voice. Peter's playing partner said, at virtually the same time, "Sit down, golf ball." The ball refused its orders, and rolled into the bunker. Peter watched in stunned, silent, and angry amazement, and then he made a bogey. There is little more reprehensible to a professional golfer than making a bogey on a par-five; the pro would rather take a double bogey on a tough par-four any day of the week. Peter was livid. The rub of the green had not been kind to him; he was unlucky that the ball did not hit the pin, unlucky to have encountered a patch of green with such a severe contour, unlucky to have the ball roll all the way into the bunker. Not that he had played a perfect shot; he played his difficult chip out of the woods just slightly too firmly and that, ultimately, was the reason it went in the bunker. But coming off the green, for some reason, he starting yelling, "Never talk to my golf ball, never talk to my golf ball, goddamnit, never talk to my golf ball." The other pro came up to me and said, "Is he talking to me, or to you?" "Me," I said. What did Peter think, that the golf ball did the *opposite* of what I asked it to? Besides, that round was our thirty-third competitive round together, and he had *never* before said *anything* to me about not talking to his golf ball, which I had been doing from the start. If he didn't want me talking to his golf ball he should have told me so much earlier. To hold me responsible for the chip shot's final resting place in the bunker was unreasonable and unfair. Moreover, to admonish me in so loud a voice, in front of another player and his caddie, was embarrassing and mean. The other caddie, very prominent in looper circles, said to me on our way to the ninth tee, "Does he always treat you like that?" It was while walking down the ninth fairway, keeping my distance from my boss, that I started to fantasize about firing Peter. *Nah, not here,* I reasoned, *too close to the clubhouse. Stick him with the bag when he's miles away.*

But that was an aberration. In the main, I liked working for Peter, and I loved being a caddie. In fact, if I did not enjoy newspaper work as much as I do, I'm quite sure I'd be a career tour caddie. By mid-term in my caddie education, I had caddied two dozen rounds in a favorite navy blue polo shirt. The shirt's left shoulder was threadbare, a reminder of the friction generated by a professional golf bag against a shoulder. I could not part with the shirt, despite Christine's requests: it was an emblem of my work.

The pleasures of the work were modest. I very much enjoyed

cleaning the clubs, getting all the dirt out of the scoring lines on the club face with a sharp tee, getting the grime off the grips with a damp towel. You'd do each grip individually, and then you'd let the club rest, grip up, against the outside top ring of a standing bag, to dry in the sun. You'd go club by club. The putter always stayed in the bag and your player always had one club in hand, so when you were finished, you had twelve clubs spaced around the bag, like the hour markings on a clock.

The greatest pleasure comes when caddie and player are in perfect synchronization. Your man asks, "How far?" You say, "One thirty-five, slight cross breeze, right to left." He says, "Just a little nine, right?" You say, "That's right." He pulls the club from the bag. While he waggles, you pick up the bag by its handle and move four yards to his right, and directly even with him. He makes a graceful swing and you hear the wonderful click, the happy union of ball and sweet spot, and the shot soars beautifully. Directly under that arc, a perfectly rectangular divot, four inches long and two inches wide, flies softly and straight out on a perfect parabola, reaching a height of five feet and landing fifteen feet in front of the player. While the ball is in the air, and you know it is green-bound because everything is right, you lay down the bag and simultaneously pull out the putter, which does not get caught up on any other clubs, and walk to the divot. You pick it up, turn around, and start walking to your man. You have the divot in your left hand and the putter in your right. By now the shot has landed on the green and your player is pleased with the result and you pass each other, starboard to starboard. You hand him his putter—either horizontally or vertically (I prefer horizontally)—and you say, "Good one," and he says, "Thanks." You return the divot to its spot, place a sneaker on the center of it, lift up your other foot, and bounce a little. You pick up the bag and throw the strap over the middle of your shoulder and walk calmly to the green. Your man has a birdie putt, and you are both pleased.

All that made the life addictive, too.

CHAPTER EIGHT

SEEKING NIRVANA

I HAVE BEEN WONDERING WHY Ian Woosnam was a better player than Peter Teravainen. Peter was as long as Woosnam and could at will hit the ball high or low or with a draw or a fade. Peter was a marvelous bunker player and in a pickle he was inventive and daring. He could chip his golf ball with precision and was an astute reader of tricky greens, especially on long putts. He was not a great close-range putter, but neither was Woosnam, and he did not sink his share of twenty-footers, but neither had Hogan. He thought his way around the golf course intelligently, he clubbed himself accurately, he prepared himself well, he had an intuitive understanding of conditions, and he generally kept his emotions under control. He could play the game well enough to make a living from it, and that alone satisfied his primary goal. But there was something else he wanted, too—a tour victory—and *that* was his grail. "If you're good enough to play out here for ten years, and you don't have a *W* next to your name, something's wrong. People know. They'll say, 'Yeah, he could play a little, but he never won.' I've been in a position to win and haven't done it. It's disturbing, but dwelling on it is worse, so you just keep on going, hoping that at the next stop it'll be your turn."

From 1982 through 1990, Peter had earned two hundred

thousand pounds at European tour events and had twice finished second. In those same years, Ian Woosnam had tour prize winnings of *two million* two hundred thousand pounds and had won eighteen European tour events. Why should there be such a discrepancy between the two? I've been trying to sort that out in my mind. My only finding is that the questions yield more questions.

First, are you certain that Teravainen is not as good as Woosnam?

Yes, the record shows it. In 1990, when Woosnam finished first on the Order of Merit, he played in seventeen tournaments, never missed a cut, had eleven top-ten finishes, including five wins, and had a stroke average of 69.66. Teravainen finished in eighty-fourth place on the 1990 Order of Merit, played in thirty-one tournaments, finished in the money in only eighteen of them, had not one top-ten finish, and had a stroke average of 72.38.

Why doesn't Teravainen score as well as Woosnam?

Because Woosnam is a better golfer.

What makes Woosnam the better golfer?

He makes more good shots and fewer bad shots than Peter.

Does that mean Woosnam can play shots that Peter cannot?

No, it doesn't. I've never seen Woosnam do anything with a golf ball that Peter can't do.

Does Woosnam practice more than Peter?

No.

Does Woosnam have a better swing?

What do you mean by 'better'?

Is it more, classical?

Yes, but so what? Raymond Floyd's swing is less conventional than Teravainen's, and he's won twenty-one U. S. tour events, including two P. G. A. Championships, a Masters, and a U. S. Open.

Is Woosnam smarter than Teravainen?

He is, in a way.

But Teravainen went to Yale, and Woosnam was finished with school by the age of sixteen.

Means nothing.

But Peter's reading all the time and has all these theories on the way the game works. Out of the blue, he comes up with these things. Remember the day he suddenly said, "The key to this game is to have your good shot come in groups of two?" He has novel thoughts. I wouldn't call Woosnam philosophical or analytical or engaging.

So?

So how is Woosnam smarter than Teravainen?

Woosnam has a genius for golf that Teravainen lacks, or at least has not yet developed.

How does that genius reveal itself?

In his shot-making, in his scoring. Assuming all the analysis is correct—you guess correctly on the wind, the bounce, the slope, the distance, the line, the club—any golf shot, including any putt, typically fails because of error in at least one of three technical areas: sometimes at impact the club face is not square to an imaginary line that runs to the target; sometimes the path of the clubhead through the ball is not the optimal one; sometimes the clubhead is not moving at the ideal speed when it meets the ball. Both Woosnam and Teravainen know what they must do, mechanically, to produce good shots. But Woosnam has fewer mechanical breakdowns than Peter because his brain is better able to instruct his body what to do. The gap between desire and reality is smaller for Woosnam than for Peter.

What else?

Ultimately, it comes down to truthfulness, of a sort. When Woosnam instructs himself to pull off a particular shot, he truly believes he can make the shot happen. There's no interference, no confusion, no guessing, just an open tunnel from his brain to his body. Teravainen tries to tell himself the same thing, but there are parts of himself that won't believe he can make a certain swing or hole a certain putt.

What parts?

The evanescent parts. The parts in which he perceives himself.

So Teravainen doesn't perceive himself as a winner?

I'm saying there is something within him that holds him back, a part that attaches more value to being an above-water journeyman touring professional than being a golf star. Early in their careers, Teravainen held up Mike Hill as a model, and Woosnam held up Tom Watson. Peter believes there is something phony and unrugged about being a star. Stars invariably start appearing in commercials and once they do they no longer make their living solely from the playing of the game. I think the very notion of stardom violates Peter's evolving Buddhist beliefs, for Buddhism rejects the caste system, on which the star system is ultimately based.

Are Buddhism and golf compatible?

Very much so, but I don't think an ardent Buddhist would make the winning of a golf tournament a goal. Buddhism teaches that sorrow ends with the end of desire, and desire ends when you have followed the Eightfold Path to Nirvana, the state of complete, blissful detachment. Following the path requires a dedication to certain types of concentration, effort, mindfulness, resolve, speech, action, employment, and belief. In golf, you have the opportunity to dedicate yourself to all those things. But if a true Buddhist were to win a golf tournament, I think it would be happenstance, something on the way to Nirvana: "I wasn't trying to beat anybody, it just worked out that way." I'd love to see a golfer in the state of Nirvana. I bet he'd be able to be the ball. Remember "be the ball," Chevy Chase's brilliant advice in *Caddyshack*?

I remember. But you said winning a golf tournament was a grail for Peter—that doesn't sound very Buddhist.

Peter has never claimed to be an ardent Buddhist. He has only said that he is learning about Buddhism; he spent his first twenty-five years as a Protestant in New England with typically Western ideas of success and failure and only started living an Eastern life in 1988, when he married Veronica, a Buddhist, in a traditional Chinese ceremony, and moved to Singapore. Give the guy a break; he must be enduring an internal revolution.

Have you ever noticed that when Peter takes off his glasses he looks Oriental?

I have.

It's curious.

It is.

Do you think Peter can become as good as Woosnam?

Definitely, but by the time he does, Woosnam may no longer be such a lofty benchmark. Throughout the world there are thousands of professional golfers, and tens of millions of amateur golfers, who wish they could play as well as Peter. Worldwide, there might be two hundred people who play better than Peter. There is the best golfer in the world and there is the worst golfer in the world and in between everybody can look both up and down. You want to look up, because if you can figure out why somebody is better, you might have a good first step to improvement. I think that's why we make these expert golfers out to be gods, and why we study their words about the swing as if they were scripture. Woosnam's got something on Peter, he knows something that Peter doesn't, but then Peter has something on Armando Saavedra, and Armando Saavedra . . .

Golf is not a game where one player "has something" on another. You don't have to be a Buddhist to see that. The game is one of individuality. Yes, the tournament golfer is playing the field, but what matters finally is what he does against the course, what he does against par, what he does against himself. In some basic way, the golfer must know himself. I would think Woosnam must know himself. Does Peter know himself?

I think he does.

That's the main thing. Know yourself, and be not afraid.

"My mind is very frail," Peter said. We were walking off the seventh tee during the third round of the Madrid Open and I had just unwittingly said something he found disturbing. He wanted to make sure that I never again committed such injudiciousness, and in explaining himself he said something I had never before known any professional athlete to be honest enough to acknowledge: "My mind is very frail."

On the fifth hole, a short par-five, Peter had become acquainted with a bush and did well to make par by getting up-and-down from a greenside bunker. Peter had been getting up-and-down out of bunkers—one shot out of a bunker, followed by a holed putt—all week. "The sand wedge is going good," Peter said as we walked to the sixth tee. The sixth, I realized silently, was an illustration of his point; in the previous two rounds, he had missed the green twice, and both times he had saved par from bunkers. "Do us a favor here," I said. "Knock it on the green."

It was a stupid thing to say. I meant only to be encouraging, but my words backfired. With a 7-iron, Peter made a tentative, lunging swing and knocked his ball into a bunker again. After playing a tricky bunker shot, he left himself a ten-footer for par, which he made for his third consecutive out-of-the-sand par on the hole. While we were walking after his tee shot on the seventh hole, Peter turned to me and said, "It's a good thing I made that putt, or we wouldn't be talking now. When you said, 'Knock it on the green,' I know you were only trying to build me up. But you did just the opposite. I'm coming off the fifth, feeling good after saving par from the bunker. I've got good thoughts going, and then you go and remind me of my past problems on the sixth. And now, instead of feeling good, I'm thinking negative thoughts. I make a bad swing and knock it in the bunker again. I'm standing in the bunker thinking, 'Maybe I don't have another save in me.' My mind is very frail."

I hadn't, of course, actually mentioned the bunkered tee shots in my comment, but his always-clicking mind discovered the buried mention of them immediately. Another player might have accepted my comment as a simple imperative: Knock it on the green. And another player might have just kissed off my remark as dumb but innocuous. Peter could not. He could not shut his brain off. After that, I understood better what Ian Bottomley told me early on, on the overnight train from St. Raphael to Port Bou, that the ultimate goal was to think about nothing at all. Maybe if you can do that you have reached golf Nirvana. But how do you get a man like Peter, with his mighty brain, to think about nothing? Could there be an Eightfold Path for golf that would funnel all the feverish thoughts bouncing about Peter's inner walls? Peter had the truthfulness necessary to become a touring professional—most of the time, he could analyze a shot realistically, tell himself what he needed to do to make the shot happen, and do it. But he also had fears that I think prevented him from reaching a higher level, fears unconnected to his evolving Buddhist beliefs. He recognized that it was possible that swing refinements could improve his game, but he was afraid of taking the chance that they might not. There were certain shots that he was wholly capable of making from which he would back off: hitting a big driver in a draw wind, hitting a 1-iron off a bare fairway lie, going after twenty-five-foot eagle putts. At some point, because of the occasional bad experience, he had convinced himself that these shots were no longer part of his repertoire, and he wouldn't do the thing he needed to do—try them again in competition so that he might regain his trust in them. Instead, he'd resist these shots, and I could understand why: his wife was pregnant, they were saving for a house, money was tight, and he was playing golf for their livelihood. I had great sympathy for his plight. The professional golfer is not like the newspaper reporter who wishes he were a novelist. The reporter can work on his book at night. The touring professional has one chance and one chance only. The shot is in front of him and the question is, *What's he going to do with it?*

In the United States, we commonly think of four major professional golf championships: the Masters, the U. S. and British Opens, and the P.G.A. Championship. But in Europe there is only passing interest in the U.S.P.G.A. Championship, while the P.G.A. Championship of the European tour is followed keenly. It is held each year in late May on the West Course of the Wentworth Club, in the tony London suburb of Virginia Water. The European tour has its offices at the Wentworth Club, at which half a dozen tour caddies (the so-called Wentworth Six) received their early training and near to which some of the top players live. In its prestige and prize money, and in the field it attracts, the P.G.A. Championship is a near-major. So you could imagine

Peter's excitement when he made the turn in the third round of the 1991 P.G.A. Championship and saw that he was two shots off the lead. Three players were tied for first at eleven under par: Wayne Riley, Bernhard Langer, and Colin Montgomerie. Jesper Parnevik, a young Swede, and Seve Ballesteros were one shot back. Richard Boxall, Gordon Brand, Jr., Woosnam, Nick Faldo, and Peter were all two shots back. On the leader board, in tall white capital letters against a blue background, the name TERAVAINEN was sandwiched right in between WOOSNAM and FALDO. That was a great sight. I remember thinking, "Could this be the week Peter does it? A big win on a famous course, outside London, and over Langer, Montgomerie, Ballesteros, and Woosnam? How perfect."

In the third round, Peter was again paired with Brian Barnes—the extravagant Scotsman with whom Peter had played in a Majorcan sandstorm eleven weeks earlier. Barnes's presence ensured a substantial and vocal gallery. Peter had an audience of his own, which included Veronica, in the fourth month of her pregnancy; Rose and Bill Malley (Peter's traveling partners from the start of the year until a hand injury forced Bill to take an injury leave from the tour in May); the Burmese owner of the flat where Peter stayed (and prayed) when he was in London (there was a Buddhist shrine in it) Christine; and Christine's friend, Catherine. The atmosphere was festive and exciting, and became more so when we made the turn—having played the front nine in three under par—and saw the leader board.

Peter's name did not last on it for very long. He made a bogey on the tenth, an uphill par-three, and he was on the leader board no more. The tournament started to unravel for him at the twelfth, a par-five playing so short that it was reachable for Peter with two irons, as firm as the fairways were: a true birdie hole. I was thinking that an eagle would get him right back into the tournament. I don't know what Peter was thinking. His drive from the hole's elevated tee was the worst I had ever seen from him: a snap hook that went forty yards into the woods. Incredibly, the ball was found—by a wandering, lost spectator who stumbled upon it amongst the twigs and the leaves. There was no shot at all, so Peter went back to the tee, adding two strokes to his score, and began again. He hit the second drive perfectly.

"Whatta we got?"

"One seventy-eight to the hole, slight helping breeze."

I had envisioned Peter taking a 6-iron, knocking it, in caddie parlance, "adjacent," and making the putt to save par. Club selection seemed obvious: a 6-iron was what he had hit in the first round, when he had 172 yards, no breeze, and that was just right. When Peter pulled an 8-iron out of the bag, I knew he and I were thinking differently. His goal was to avoid the hazards that a wildly errant shot could bring into play: a stream well to the left of the green, and an out-of-bounds beyond it. Peter was not feeling particularly good about his accuracy just then, and he was taking no chances. He hit the 8-iron short of the green, pitched on, and two-putted for a double-bogey seven on the twelfth, a hole where the field was averaging well under five strokes. Then he made bogeys on the fifteenth, sixteenth, and seventeenth holes, and he was never in contention after that. He had it going, and then it died. The strangest thing was that except for the duck hook off the twelfth tee, he didn't hit bad shots. He just couldn't score. It was as if he were trapped in a nightmare, running on a treadmill with which he could not keep up. Why did he hit such a poor drive on twelve? Because at impact the club face of his driver was not square to the imaginary line that runs to the target. Why did that happen? Because he started his downswing before he finished his backswing. Why did that happen? Because he was anxious. All right, fine, he was anxious; he probably recognized that before he started the swing. But he's been a professional golfer for twelve years, he knows, intimately, exactly what he has to do to make a good swing, anxious or not, so why couldn't he do it? Why couldn't he make the swing he wanted to make, the swing he has made successfully thousands of times before? What was the nature of the brain-to-body interference, and how could it have been prevented? Why did his game, which was so solid and so good for the first forty-five holes, and for the final eighteen holes, fall apart in that one nine-hole stretch, on the back nine of the third round? I don't know, and I don't think

Peter knows. Something spooked him, deep inside, somewhere inaccessible.

Only the results were tangible. He finished in a tie for thirteenth.

Players on the European tour routinely go weeks, sometimes months, without seeing their wives, and then have periods when they see them constantly. For most married couples, this arrangement would not resemble normal life, but it is the only schedule that Peter and Veronica have ever known, so it seemed normal to them. When Veronica was at home in Singapore and Peter was out on tour, he would call about once a week, and even that was pushing their budget. When they had time together, they both valued it. Veronica traveled with Peter for three weeks during the 1991 season, at the P. G. A. Championship and the two tournaments after it, the British Masters, in Woburn, and the Murphy's Cup, in York. Veronica, who speaks fluent English with a Chinese accent, is a diminutive and charming woman whose presence plainly affected Peter. With Veronica around, Peter was more social and patient, and he practiced more. He also ate better. That was because nutrition was one of Veronica's particular interests. She brought Peter a special nutritional supplement from Singapore, made from an ancient Chinese recipe she learned from her mother. "You know how birds use saliva as a glue to hold together their nests? The saliva is good for you," she explained to me. "We boil the nests, slowly in shallow water, and drink the extract. It gives you strength." Peter said the stuff worked.

Peter met Veronica when he was playing in a golf tournament in Singapore in 1986, and before her pregnancy she caddied for him whenever her schedule as a flight attendant cooperated. But nobody ever confused her with a golf expert. She was more like a golf expert in reverse. If Peter was unsure which of two putters to use, he would ask Veronica for her preference, and then use the putter that she had rejected.

Veronica caddied for Peter at the 1989 British Open at Royal Troon, and that proved to be memorable for both of them. The night before the third round, Peter left the dinner table to call the championship office and find out his tee time. "Your time is 10:05," he was told, "and you're playing with Jack Nicklaus."

Big names don't normally cause Peter to quake. He's been paired with just about everybody. He's played with Tom Watson. He's played with Greg Norman. He's played with Ian Woosnam. But Nicklaus was different. Nicklaus was the king; Nicklaus had redefined the game. Nicklaus was other-worldly. Peter had never considered drawing Nicklaus as a partner before. He put the phone down on the cradle and stared at it. For a moment, he was numb. He called right back; he couldn't remember his tee time. His skin got clammy. He gathered all the coolness he could muster, returned to the table, and said, "I got our time. We're off at five past ten." He caught his breath. "And we're playing with Nicklaus."

"Oh," Veronica said, "that's nice."

"Jack Nicklaus."

"Yes."

"The greatest player of all time," Peter said.

"Very nice," Veronica said.

Peter didn't sleep a wink. Veronica had no trouble at all.

The next morning, on the practice putting green, Teravainen walked over to Nicklaus and introduced himself. Jack was cordial. Peter warned Nicklaus about Veronica. "She doesn't know much about golf. If she's in your way at all, just tell me." Nicklaus was amused. The two golfers chatted. Peter explained how he had come to marry a woman from Singapore.

Walking down the first fairway, Nicklaus turned to Veronica and said, "I consider myself something of an expert on the Orient, and I would say, looking at your features and studying your accent, that you must be from Singapore."

Veronica stared at him in amazement. "How'd you know that, how'd you do that?" she innocently asked.

Nicklaus revealed nothing, and to this day Veronica thinks of Nicklaus as a man of extraordinary perception. He chatted with her all the way around the course and in the process won over another fan. When Veronica and I talked about Nicklaus, she spoke glowingly of him.

Peter remembers every shot both he and Nicklaus took in that round, which is unusual for him, and everything Nicklaus said. Walking to the second green, Nicklaus said to Teravainen, "So, Peter, what are you reading?"

They, too, chatted pleasantly through the round (Peter had the feeling that the Nicklaus of a decade or two or three earlier would have been far more taciturn). They talked about golf in the United States and about golf in Europe. They talked about books. They talked about colleges. But Nicklaus said not one word to Peter about his game, until the green of the par-four eighteenth hole.

Peter hit a poor drive and a poor second, to the right of a nasty greenside bunker. His ball was sitting on firm ground and the hole on the home green was cut just beyond the bunker. Peter had two choices: he could play something very tricky, trying to nudge his ball just over the bunker, down a hill, and to the hole, or he could hit a conservative shot—a little pitch to the center of the green. Teravainen was playing with a three-time British Open champion and the most accomplished player in the game's history; the gallery was enormous; Peter was on TV. What should he do? Try the risky, potentially spectacular shot, or cut his losses and play safe?

Teravainen played the safe shot. As he passed Nicklaus on the green, the Golden Bear said, "That was a good play from over there." Teravainen was stunned: Nicklaus was suggesting that he would have done the very same thing! Peter finished with a bogey, and Nicklaus's 71 was a shot better than Peter's card. But Teravainen was not disappointed. He regards that intriguing comment from Nicklaus as the most meaningful compliment he has ever received on any shot he has ever made. He will never forget it. He regards the round as one of the most memorable of the thousands of competitive rounds he has played. The day was made even more special to him because his wife was there to share in it, just as Jack Nicklaus, Jr., as caddie, was able to share in his father's stirring win in the 1986 Masters. Veronica may not have immediately understood the nuances of Nicklaus's final comment to Peter, but she witnessed it. Nobody can ever tell Peter that he never played with Nicklaus. All he has to do is ask his wife. They experienced that remarkable day together.

Over the course of our five months together, I had grown very fond of Peter. I loved watching him line up putts. He would stand halfway between the ball and the hole, just off the line of the putt, put his hands on his hips for symmetry and balance, and then strangely throw his shoulders and head way back and shake his head from side to side as if he were watching a tennis match, with a contorted face that said, "Goddamnit, I've got to find out what this putt does." He always tried so hard! I felt I was, next to Veronica, his biggest supporter, and I was always wishing I could do more.

On the long drive from Monte Carlo to Gleneagles for the Scottish Open, Christine and I thought about staying with the tour. After the Scottish Open came the British Open, followed by tournaments in Holland, Sweden, Germany, and Switzerland. It sounded so inviting. Every week we were becoming a little more ingenious in our traveling, and we were surviving on the combination of caddie wages and freelance writing. But as we entered Scotland and drove through East Lothian on our way to Gleneagles, past the links of Dunbar and North Berwick and Muirfield and Gullane, I found myself feeling envious of the people who were actually playing, and I felt a strong yearning to play again. Scotland, where the game and the business of caddying originated, was the right place to retire as a caddie and to resume my playing career. After the Scottish Open, we decided, we would go to the British Open—at Royal Birkdale in Southport, England—but only as spectators. After that, we'd go straight back to Scotland. I had told Peter about my pending retirement a month before the Scottish Open. In the meantime, I was hoping to leave the caddie ranks with a bang; I was hoping for nothing less than a Teravainen win in the Scottish Open.

Nature conspired against us. The weather for the entire week was miserable, but we caught the worst of it. In the morning of the first round, it was windy and cold, but in the afternoon it was windier and colder, and it was raining, and that's when we played. Peter shot level par in the first round, and played extremely well to do that. The cold, wind, and rain continued throughout the morning of the second round, and Peter continued to play extremely well, as well, in fact, as he had played in all our time together. He came to the last hole—a challenging 522-yard par-five lined with bunkers—one over par for the round. He thought that if he made a par he would have a chance to make the cut and if he made a birdie he definitely would. From the tee he daringly decided to hit driver, bringing bunkers into play but giving himself a chance to reach the green in two shots. He hit the driver well, leaving himself 221 yards for his second shot. With a 4-iron, he knocked his ball on the green, about thirty-five feet from the hole. His first putt stopped four feet from the hole. "I left us some work," he said after marking his ball and seeking protection under the umbrella. "This one's going straight in," I said. It did—a birdie to finish, even par for thirty-six holes in extreme conditions. Peter was playing excellently. Who could say what phenomenal third and fourth rounds would bring? I felt victory was still in sight.

Later that evening, I was at the George Hotel in Edinburgh, attending something called "A Scottish Evening" with Christine and her parents, who were on a summer tour of the British Isles. Haggis was served. Bagpipes were played. Ballads were sung. Robert Burns was recited. Clans, kilts, and tartans were explained. A pleasant evening. I slipped out at one point to call the tournament office for Peter's third-round tee time.

"Teravainen, Teravainen—I don't see that name at all. What score is he on," the voice on the other end of the phone said.

"Level par," I answered.

"Oh, level? That's the problem, then. The cut came in at one under."

The haggis suddenly felt like lead in my stomach. I felt myself sinking.

"Yes, weather cleared up nicely in the afternoon, and the scores came way down. One under is your cut."

My caddie career had ended with a thud.

CHAPTER NINE

MAGIC

FOR TERAVAINEN, career and life carried on. That's the nature of tournament golf. Every week is a fresh start. Four days after the missed cut at the Scottish Open, Peter had set up shop at the Southport and Ainsdale Golf Club, where he competed in the two-day British Open qualifying tournament, the testing ground for the rank-and-file touring professional who seeks a place in the British Open. If Peter succeeded there, he would be playing in the oldest golf championship in the world, and, in the minds of most non-Americans, the most significant. That's why they call it the "Open." I went looking for Peter at Southport and Ainsdale, because I wanted to show support for his cause, and because I wanted to say thank you and good-bye. Our abrupt finish in Scotland had robbed me of that chance.

It was strange to see his bag on the back of another caddie. I derived a sort of perverse pleasure watching another looper struggling to keep up with Teravainen's coffee-aided pace. The caddie's name was also Michael—he was called Irish Mike, a middle-aged, hard-working man with the physique of a welterweight. I knew Irish Mike, a veteran caddie who pitched a tent week after week, and I liked him, but I found myself watching him with a critical eye. When I saw him talking to Peter, post-bogey, all the way from a green to the next tee, I said to myself, "What's this guy doing? You don't talk *now.* Peter'll blow him off any second." But as they walked, it seemed that Peter was listening intently, and when they reached the tee, I saw Peter laugh, a genuine laugh, and I'd be untruthful if I didn't tell you that I felt a twinge of jealousy: I had been replaced.

That night, after the first round of the qualifier, Peter and I had dinner at a place called Mama Mia Pizzeria, in Southport. I asked Peter if he had been stunned, as I was, when he learned that our two-day total of even par was not good enough to make the cut in Scotland. "Not really," he said. "When I saw the weather improving through the afternoon, I had a feeling that level par might not hold up." I asked him if he had found the missed cut at Gleneagles particularly disappointing, as I had, since he had played so well. "Not really," he said. "When you play as well as you can, and it's not enough, there's not much to be disappointed about. You've done all you can do. I just got in the car and drove straight here for a practice round." That was when I realized that the Scottish Open had held added significance only for me. I was in the midst of a golfing adventure; everything had added meaning. For Peter, it was another week in a golfing *life.*

Peter asked about my plans, and I told him that after the Open Christine and I would be returning to Scotland. We discussed some Scottish courses Peter had played, courses he had come to know not on pleasure trips, but at Open qualifiers. When the Open is at Muirfield, there's a qualifier at North Berwick. When the Open is played at Troon, there's one at Barassie. When the Open is played on the Old Course in St. Andrews, there's a qualifier on the Lundin Links. Peter would not do what I was about to do: make an extensive trip through Scotland simply to *play.* "When you play professional golf you lose the ability to play simply for fun. If I'm playing a practice round, and I hit a 2-iron just perfectly, I don't get a buzz. I get nothing. Unless it happens in a tournament, in competition, it doesn't mean a thing. You're lucky, because you're able to enjoy the game in ways that I no longer can. For me, golf is always equated with money. For good or for bad, at this point the two are inseparable."

Financially, Peter and I had had a successful campaign together. With the season about two-thirds of the way completed, Peter had made forty-three thousand pounds and was well on his way to having the most lucrative year of his career. He was number forty-six on the Order of Merit. (In the previous year, he had finished eighty-fourth and had won fifty-two thousand pounds.) He was among the statistical leaders in driving distance. He was playing his best golf since 1984, the year he finished fifteenth on the Order of Merit and won forty thousand pounds. I had the feeling that his stature among his colleagues had improved over the course of the season: making a decent paycheck week after week does that. I knew his stature among the caddies had ascended. When word of my retirement got loose, caddies were all over him, looking for work. I asked Peter if he would return to his old system—occasionally hiring a tour caddie, more often taking a local caddie, other times keeping the caddie work within the family (Veronica, himself). He said he didn't think so.

"Having a regular caddie has helped me this year," he said. I was flattered: that was the most direct compliment he had ever paid me. "I'd like to work with a guy on a steady basis, if I found a guy I liked." Irish Mike was not a candidate—he had a regular job with Christy O'Connor, Jr. We discussed some caddies, and what Peter would have to pay to retain them. "I could raise my wage, to keep a guy I really liked," Peter said. Had I heard that right? "Sometimes you have to spend money to make money," Peter said. I was amazed.

I only hoped that that did not signify more substantive change. The last time I saw Peter was on the eve of the 1991 British Open (for which he had qualified), standing at the Tommy Armour Golf Company booth, set up on the Open grounds. The marketing people at Tommy Armour, an American golf club manufacturer named for the stylish Scottish-born winner of the 1927 U. S. Open and the 1931 British Open, were trying to strengthen their position outside the United States. They wanted Peter to play their clubs. A couple of outings a year in Singapore and in Europe stood to be part of the deal, and there would be, no doubt, some corporate schmoozing along the way. Peter was considering it. I wondered if Peter would succumb to the pressures of an expanding family and a planned house purchase. Had Teravainen's priorities changed? The Tommy Armour people had given him some clothes. I saw Peter wearing a pastel blue cotton sweater, sheer and delicate—a very fine sweater. I thought he looked uncomfortable in it.

"You give us a few years, Teravainen," said a marketing man in the booth, "we'll give you a complete make-over."

Peter smiled, a thin smile that did not reveal his tiny teeth. I wondered if Peter's standards were in jeopardy. I tried to remember the last time I had seen him in his favorite pants, the slate gray shiny ones with the off-white pinstriping. Had he worn them in Scotland? I thought he had. Yes, I was quite sure that he had. As long as those trousers were still in circulation, I felt sure there was nothing to worry about.

The Ballesteros I saw at the Open was not the Ballesteros I had seen in Majorca, when he was getting free swing counsel from every Tom, Dick, and Vijay, when he had to bounce one out of a pond to make the cut in his own tournament. The real Seve started to emerge the following week, in Tarragona. That's where he faced a 245-yard second shot on a par-five, over water and off a tight lie, and he elected to hit driver. This was not the club his new caddie, Billy Foster, would have chosen. But Billy was still learning the mysterious ways of his boss: Ballesteros, a man of great pride, superstition, and stubbornness, was trying to exorcise a golfing devil from his body, and attempting improbable shots was part of the rite. He hit that shot poorly, and it found the water, but the result was irrelevant. The important thing was the attempt. He was trying to return the long-carrying, driver-off-a-tight-lie shot to his artillery. He knew that the golfer who could make such a shot still lurked somewhere within him. He was just temporarily subjugated by an evil force.

The exorcism must have worked. Or maybe it was the lesson

from David Leadbetter, the golf-healer. *Something* happened, because in the weeks and months after Tarragona, Ballesteros started playing amazing golf. He played decently in the Masters, in April. Then, in May and June, using a new driver (metal, replacing wood), a new putter (a Tad Moore, replacing his old Ping), and a new putting thought (Leadbetter told him to stand more open to the line of the putt), he went wild. After the Masters, he traveled to Japan to play in two tournaments. In the first event, he finished second. In the second tournament, he faced a twenty-foot putt on the seventy-second hole for victory. "This must go in," he told himself, for a missed putt would have meant a playoff, and a missed flight, and another twenty-four hours in Japan, which did not jibe with his overburdened schedule. He made the putt, won the tournament, caught his Tokyo-Madrid flight, and arrived in time for the Spanish Open, another tournament orchestrated by his company, Amen Corner. He fared much better than he had in Majorca. At the Spanish Open, he and Eduardo Romero (a dashing Argentine who plays a junior version of the Ballesteros game) finished the four rounds in a tie for the lead, and their sudden-death playoff was not settled until the seventh extra hole, where Romero made a birdie to win. In Ballesteros's next appearance, two weeks later at the P.G.A. Championship at Wentworth, he and Colin Montgomerie finished the four rounds tied for the lead. Another sudden-death playoff. On the first extra hole, Ballesteros hit a low hook off the tee, which bounced generously off a golf cart sitting in the rough and back to the fairway. He seized the moment. From 220 yards, Seve drilled a 5-iron to three feet, made birdie to Montgomerie's par, and won the tournament. In the following week, at the British Masters in Woburn, Ballesteros scared off the field and won by three shots.

After the Woburn win, Seve came into the press tent for an *en masse* interview. The room was humming: Ballesteros was back. He had shot 66, 66, 68 in the first three rounds, giving himself a seven-shot lead after fifty-four holes, then closed with a lackadaisical 75 to win by three. Ballesteros apologized for not playing better in the finale. He said it was hard to concentrate with so big a lead. "I cannot shoot every day 66," he said. "I am not God."

When the reporters on deadline were through with him, and after he signed autographs for tournament officials, and after he posed for photographs with the British Masters trophy, I worked Ballesteros into a quiet corner. Outside, it was a wintry day. Ballesteros wore two navy cashmere sweaters. He reeked of success, but I do not mean that in a material sense. The sprawling tented quarters in which we stood could not contain him. I asked him why he was playing better, and this is what he said:

"Golf is a game of moods. I had one mood from 1976 through 1986, a mood of great confidence and great optimism. I always felt aggressive, I always had a great deal of self-control, I always felt I would get good bounces. Then in 1986, even though I won six tournaments, I didn't win the one I wanted, the one I felt I was destined to win: the Masters. The tournament was mine to win and somehow the victory slipped away. After that, I didn't feel so invincible. My conquering moods came and went. In 1987, I was down. In 1988, I was up; I won the Open, I won at Westchester, I won four others. The next year, so-so—I won three times, but no majors. Then last year was the worst. I was pessimistic. I believed that if something could go wrong, it would go wrong. I started thinking of high numbers, not low numbers. I thought there was the devil in me. I said, 'Where has the confidence gone? Where has the optimism gone?' It hadn't left me. It was *inside* me, but I could not bring it out. It was trapped. I had gone over a year without winning—a very long time.

"Then at Augusta this year, things started changing. I don't know why, but they did. You make one good swing, something suddenly clicks. I don't know how it starts, but I know where. In the mind. The mind controls the heart. The heart controls the body. By the second week in Japan, I started to feel like I could do anything. That is how I used to feel all the time.

"I am very happy now, not because I have won a tournament, not because I have won three of my last four tournaments. I am happy because I am again playing well the game that I love. I am happy because the feelings are back, the feelings of confidence and optimism. I did not know if they were going to come back. In some ways the mood is the same as when I was a young man, and in some ways it is different. Now I am more aware of the mood and how special it is, and I understand that it can come and go. I appreciate the mood more. I have the maturity to enjoy it.

"The moment of victory is nice, but it is not the moment I live for. I am happiest when I am in the hunt for the title—that is the moment of total excitement for me. I am like the gambler. The great moment is not when the roulette wheel has finished spinning, and the gambler knows if he has won or lost. The great moment comes while the wheel is spinning, and he does not yet know the outcome. That is what I live for."

With the win at Woburn, Ballesteros was on top of the Order of Merit, and at the top of his game. Although the long, lush grasses of the U. S. Open took their annual toll—he missed the cut by two shots—he returned to Europe and continued to play well: an eighth-place finish in the Monte Carlo Open followed by a tenth-place finish at the Scottish Open. He was the talk of the tour. He had made his very name exciting again. With the Open at Birkdale—the place Ballesteros had revealed his golfing genius to the world as a nineteen-year-old in 1976—golf people were buzzing again about The Great Man. The bookmakers were sending him off at five-to-one. Only Faldo, going off at seven-to-two, was more heavily favored. After Ballesteros came Woosnam, at eight-to-one, followed by Payne Stewart, the new U. S. Open champion, at sixteen-to-one. (Teravainen was being offered at one-hundred-to-one.) By the time of the Open, Billy Foster had developed a much greater understanding of his boss.

On the eighteenth green of the first round of the 1991 Open, Ballesteros (playing with Johnny Miller, the man who had defeated him for the Open title in 1976) faced a forty-five-foot putt for birdie. Ballesteros was not thinking in terms of holing the putt, even though it would have given him the outright lead to the championship. Even for Ballesteros, such a thought would have been audacious, considering the fifteen paces worth of bumpy terrain his ball had to traverse, considering that his fingers were numb from the cold and the wind. In those conditions, you take two putts, and you are pleased. Even Seve. But for some odd reason his caddie saw the putt as holeable. "Knock it in," Billy said to Ballesteros as they reviewed the putt. "Strange things happen sometimes." The stands around the eighteenth green, the very green where Ballesteros had performed magic fifteen years earlier, were packed. Every window in the clubhouse was filled with faces and craned necks. A bobby with no interest or background in golf was suddenly enthralled. While Ballesteros stood over his putt, the enormous crowd paid its respect with a huge, eerie silence, and a total stillness. And then, an eruption—Ballesteros had made the putt! He had a first-round 66, and he was leading the Open.

Ballesteros didn't waste any time in the press tent. He came in, made a few comments about his game, and left. He didn't want to answer a litany of questions. He didn't want to analyze. He didn't want to hear analyses. He didn't want to talk about metal woods or David Leadbetter or his new putting stance. He knew what was going on and so did the reporters: *The Great Man had rediscovered his magic!*

PART TWO

COMING IN

He began to get pars, as the whitecaps flashed on one side of the links and on the other the wine-red electric commuter trains swiftly glided up to Glasgow and back. This was happiness, on this wasteland between the tracks and the beach, and freedom, of a wild and windy sort.

—John Updike, "FARRELL'S CADDIE"

CHAPTER TEN

STARK

"TELL ME PRECISELY WHAT IT IS YOU SEEK TO ACCOMPLISH," John Stark said. We were sitting in his crammed office, in the back of his pro shop at the Crieff Golf Club, in central Scotland. I was expecting a trim man in a tweed coat, but my expectations were wrong. Stark was a behemoth, two or three inches over six feet and a stone or two over two hundred pounds, with a deep, booming voice and a rich Scots dialect. He wore white loafers, shiny blue nylon sweat pants, and a white golf shirt a size or two too small. Around his neck hung a gold chain, and the borders of his front teeth were lined with gold, too. He had a heavy, compassionate face, and thick white hair combed off his broad forehead. He smoked a cheap cigar. He was sixty years old, and he looked it, except in his eyes—he had ageless, piercing, wise blue eyes.

"I want to get better," I said quietly.

Stark stared at me. My God, how he stared at me! I felt as if the master teacher were looking right into my golfing past: here I am in an eighth-grade gym class, my first brush with the game, whacking balls with wild, happy abandon off Astroturf mats; here I am in the summer before my freshman year of college, at the height of my modest powers, which is to say, able to break eighty from time to time on a course I knew intimately; here I am, ten years later, at dangerous Pine Valley, in New Jersey, losing balls and putting monstrously while mentally composing a letter of apology to my host; here I am a few years later, on the practice tee of a Palm Beach resort, hearing old Mr. Hartmann say to the youth working the range, "Young sir, I am running out of time," and feeling solidarity with him. No, Stark wasn't staring at me, he was staring right through me: he saw my suffering, my dissatisfaction, my false pride, my humiliation, my longing, my urgency.

He lit his cigar and we sat in silence for a long moment. In time, he spoke; I remember the weird way his lips started moving, well before his words came out. I will tell you what he said, but before I do, I'd like to explain how I found my way to that back room, amid the boxed shoes waiting for feet, the unfinished woods waiting for paint, the naked shafts waiting for grips; I think I should tell you how I came to have an audience with Mr. J. M. Stark, golf professional, whose dangerous and powerful vision was so immediately apparent.

I had been looking for a teacher. In my mind, I was a seventies shooter in the midst of a thirteen-year slump, but in reality I had to play well to shoot 82, and more often shot 92. I could play to my handicap, twelve or thirteen, only on my good days, and that was an unsatisfying way to go through life. I longed to feel again the thrill of discovery, the thrill of improvement. I felt I needed a fresh start, and a teacher to set me on a new course. A British Ryder Cup player from the Palmer era, whom I had met in England while caddying for Teravainen, told me about Stark. "He teaches no two people the same way, and he knows the game from the outside and the inside," I was told. "He's a mystic, something of a recluse, and if you get him to take you on you'll be lucky indeed."

Intrigued, I wrote to John Stark, and inquired about becoming a pupil. He invited me in for a "little chat"—that's how he put it. So, during the weekend of the Scottish Open, after Peter had missed the cut, I went up to see Stark at the club where he has worked since 1961, in the town of Crieff, on the same latitude as St. Andrews, but far off the coast, midway between Loch Earn and the Firth of Tay. I left my clubs behind; I didn't want to appear presumptuous.

"You want to get better, a worthy goal," Stark said. "But what makes you think tuition is the way to improvement? I've seen many players ruined with instruction, I've seen instruction rob a player of all his natural instincts for the game."

Stark leaned back in his desk chair, which was too small to accommodate him. I didn't know if he wanted me to respond. The rhythms of Scottish and American conversation are different. The Scots pause more, and ask more questions, questions not always meant to be answered. I waited, and eventually Stark continued.

"When I was a boy, there was no teaching of golf in Scotland, not in a formal sense, and I don't think the quality of the play in this country was any worse for it. Your father showed you a couple of things when you played with him in the summer evenings. You caddied, and if you had a player you liked, you emulated him. If you were lucky enough to see a Henry Cotton, you didn't ask him how many knuckles of his left hand were visible at address. You'd follow him around, watch how he approached the game, watch his swing, and then you'd try to do the same. You'd fiddle around, perform experiments, amalgamate what he was doing with your own ideas, and come up with something distinctly your own."

A young shop assistant came in with instant coffee and Stark stirred it with a letter opener.

"You Americans have made the game so bloody mechanical and plodding. You've made these mechanical courses, where all you do is hit the ball from point A to point B. Target golf, aye, they got that name just right. The best of your countrymen have become good golf robots, outstanding golf robots, all swinging the club the same way. You've made us change the way we think about the game. As a result, there's virtually nobody left playing golf in the old Scottish manner: fast and unschooled. Not that long ago, Scottish golf had a style all its own—low, running hooks into the wind; quick, flat, handsy swings; wristy putting; bunker play where you nipped the ball cleanly; putting from twenty yards off the green; bump-and-run shots from *anywhere.* It was great fun, great *sport,* to play that way, but it wasn't very efficient. You could be impressive, but it didn't necessarily result in low scores. Of course, for a very long time we didn't care much about scores.

"That is another American thing, this fascination with score, always keeping track with pencil and scorecard. In the Scottish game, the only thing that mattered was your match, and you knew how that stood intuitively. Now you have all these endless first-tee discussions about handicaps and what type of wager to make and where the strokes should be allocated. Too much."

The telephone rang, and Stark made arrangements for a fishing trip.

"You showed us that there's money in golf. That had never occurred to us. The money has corrupted us, all of us, myself included. Once you start making it, it's a damn cancer, the money is. You start thinking, 'What can I do to make more money?' In my generation, we went into golf with no expectation of wealth. The golf alone sustained us. For years, we resisted thinking of golf as a business. Right through the Second World War, we had clubs with one full-time employee: he gave lessons, made clubs and sold 'em, kept the caddies in line, and mixed the drinks. The game was cheap then: you might have paid five quid for a year's worth of golf, and you got your money's worth. You played after work, until you could see the ball no more. You played every day, except Sunday; the Presbyterians wouldn't hear of golf on Sunday. But you played the six other days, and you hoped for wind to make your game interesting. Scotland was poor, and there was nothing else to do, except the pubs. Golf was the national sport. Everybody played. Your mother played. Golf was the game."

He took a long sip of coffee and stared me down, not a hint of smile on his face. He was sizing me up, trying to figure out if I knew what he was talking about. I was transfixed.

"In 1953, Scottish golf took a mortal blow, when Hogan came to Carnoustie to play in the Open. He had already won the Masters. He had won your Open. If I hadn't witnessed what he did at Carnoustie, I would not have believed it. I was playing in the championship, but I felt we were in different tournaments altogether. I remember how he played the sixth, a par-five. I was a reasonably long hitter, but I never regarded the hole as reachable in two, because of the fairway bunkers that came into play if you hit a big driver off the tee. I thought you had to play short of the bunkers. We all did. But Hogan showed us we were wrong. He found this little strip of fairway, between the rough and the bunkers, maybe ten yards wide, and he landed his drives on that strip every time, and from there the green could be fetched. Nobody else would have dared such a tee shot. We were amazed. They started calling that little landing zone 'Hogan's Alley.' I had never seen a technique like that before, a technique that could produce long shots that went so straight. None of us had. That was the beginning of the end of Scottish golf, in the classical sense. Hogan was playing a different game. Everybody was fascinated. Everybody became keen to study it. Everybody started thinking about method. What was Hogan's method? How could we achieve the ideal method?

"After Hogan's triumph at Carnoustie—and that is what it was—the shutterbug descended upon golf. Suddenly, there was this fascination with high-speed golf photography that enabled you to break down the swing into hundreds of stop-action photos. It all seemed so obvious: there was a correct position for *everything,* at all points in the swing. You just had to match yourself up with the pictures, make sure your angles, or your student's angles, matched the angles in the pictures. The swing, as a whole, was subverted. The important thing was all the hundreds of little movements. Every frame of Hogan showed the perfect position, for that split-second."

At this point, Stark produced a pad from a desk drawer and found a pen with the top chewed off and started drawing lines and curves with much more care than the sputtering pen could convey. While he drew, he talked.

"You know that a line, in mathematics, is in fact a series of points? Most people see only the line, but the mathematician can see the points. That's what happened with the golf swing. We teachers became mathematicians, seeing all these bloody points, but we lost track of the line. I was as guilty as anyone. I turned my back on the Scottish game, the game of my youth. A year after Hogan won at Carnoustie, I went to Sweden to teach golf there, and for my seven years there I taught a very technical game. Used photographs all the time. It made great sense to me then, made sense to me for years afterwards. Now I'm not so sure. With all this technical instruction, I don't see people playing better, and I certainly don't see them enjoying their golf more, not at any level. I see them enjoying it less. I see more frustration and less pleasure. That's what saddens me. If I stand for anything at this point in my life, it's to turn back the hands of time, to see if I can help people to treat golf as a game.

"You come to me and say you want to get better, that you want to take lessons from me, but I wonder if you really need them. You have been doing just the right thing, haven't you: working as a caddie, seeing up close world-class players, the Henry Cottons of your day. This is a very good thing. Think of the players you really admire. Right now, go on and think of them. Think of what makes them special to you. Adopt from them what is useful to yourself."

We again sat in silence for a moment. I thought of Teravainen, how his face got all scrunched up when he was trying to figure out the line of a putt, how hard he would try. I thought of the rhythmic pounding of Ballesteros's swing, a swing that reminded me of the crashing of a mighty Pacific roller.

"Who've you got in mind?" Stark asked.

"Peter Teravainen and Seve," I said.

"Interesting," Stark said. He relit his cigar. "And why do you particularly admire them?" I wanted to answer well; I felt that if I could show Stark that I was a student of the game, that the game was as important to me as it was to him, that I was worthy of his time, then maybe he would take me on. I knew that he would be unlike any other teacher I would find anywhere else. When he spoke of the mortal blow Hogan had dealt old-school Scottish golf it was without cynicism or despair. It was with reverence and fascination. It was with the tone Cronkite once reserved for the Apollo liftoffs. Through Stark, I felt, I could reincarnate myself as a Scottish golfer. I could have a fresh start.

I struggled to put together the words of my answer. *What is it that I particularly admire about Teravainen?*

Finally, I answered. "Everything Teravainen has accomplished in the game has come by way of physical effort."

"Yes, that's right, isn't it," Stark said. "You can see that in his scores. I've followed Teravainen for years—his Finnish name has always interested me—and I see that he is an exceptional par-shooter, regardless of the course, regardless of the weather. That tells you that he may lack brilliance, but that he is tough, that he knows how to make par hole after hole, round after round, week after week, year after year. Yes, Teravainen—interesting. And why Ballesteros—what do you particularly admire about him?"

"Ballesteros's game seems to come from inside him," I said. "He seems to produce shots by subconscious force, by will. Seve doesn't seem to be aware of what he is doing, he just does it. He is the opposite of Peter in that."

"Ah, very good, Michael. Yes, will is the thing with Seve. There is no one in his class today. Nick Faldo may be a better player, but Ballesteros is a better golfer. He may be the last of the Scottish players. I could watch him all day. He came here a few days ago to put on an exhibition for the kids. They were fascinated by him, as if he were a magician, which of course he is. He said to one boy, 'I don't like your swing, but I like how your ball goes.' In style he is completely different, but Ballesteros is the first player since Hogan that I have found totally mesmerizing. Good choices, those two. Now what have you learned from Teravainen that you can apply to your own game?"

It dawned on me that Stark was giving me a lesson. We were sitting in his office, surrounded by clubs. Though we had none in hand, he was giving me a lesson.

"Peter understands the value of every shot, he understands that all shots count equally," I said. "He never lets up, because he knows that one slipup will fast lead to another. He has this idea, which I think he got from Nicklaus, that when he stands over a shot he knows it will be the only time in his entire life that he is able to play that shot. After the shot is played, the moment is lost forever. So every shot is important, every shot is once-in-a-lifetime. He feels an obligation to make something of it. At the root of all his effort is great concentration. I very seldom can focus intensely on each shot through eighteen holes."

"Now there's your first mistake, Michael. Don't tell me what you can't do. What's past is prologue. Tell me what you *want* to do." I nodded; I understood. "You want to do like Teravainen, and concentrate on each shot. A worthy goal."

Stark clasped his thick hands behind his head. He was enjoying this discourse, I felt. "Now what about Ballesteros, what did you learn from him that you can apply to your own game?"

"Seve makes the most beautiful swings," I said, "so graceful and powerful. He's fluid, uncluttered. I would love to make swings like that. On the practice tee, you can see he thinks about a lot of technical things, but you don't see that on the course. He seems to be thinking only about the ball and the hole. I would hope someday to have a fluid swing like that."

"You will, when you come to trust yourself," Stark said. "Seve looks uncluttered because he trusts his mechanics. He trusts his mechanics because he knows they're good. He knows they're good because he's had successful results with them in the past." He paused. "Sometimes the game seems so simple."

Stark stood up and walked awkwardly to a window—a damaged and arthritic hip and spine had robbed him of mobility, made sitting in one place for long periods painful, and ended his days of walking eighteen holes. He stayed with the game through teaching, reading, thinking, and talking. He leaned up against the window and watched a cold early July rain fall, watched the trees shake. People were playing.

"This rain keeps up, our greens will look like bloody gargoyles," Stark said. He pulled and pressed on different parts of his face to show the softness of the greens and to imitate a gargoyle. In the shop, two or three people were waiting to see Stark.

"For how long will you be in Scotland?" he asked.

"Through the end of summer," I said.

"That's good, you've given yourself enough time to discover some of our secrets."

My time with Stark was drawing to a close. I gathered my things, happy for our excellent conversation, disappointed that he seemed unwilling to take me on as a pupil.

I was standing in the doorway to his office when Stark said, "Do you know what I mean when I say *linksland?* Linksland is the old Scottish word for the earth at the edge of the sea—tumbling, duney, sandy, covered by beach grasses. When the light hits it, and the breeze sweeps over it, you get every shade of green and brown, and always, in the distance, is the water. The land was long considered worthless, except to the shepherds and their sheep and the rabbits, and to the early golfers. You see, the game comes out of the ocean, just like man himself! Investigate our linksland, Michael, get to know it. I think you'll find it worthwhile. Drop in on your travels. I'll be curious to know what you learn."

CHAPTER ELEVEN

CRADLE

I HEEDED STARK'S WORD. After seeing him, Christine and I went to the British Open, and then straight to St. Andrews, the place of pilgrimage for theologians, academicians, and golfers, an ancient town built on the sandy shores of St. Andrews Bay, in the Kingdom of Fife. We arrived in St. Andrews at three in the afternoon on July 22, a Monday, and by five we had found a four-bedroom flat, above a hair salon on South Street, that we could afford to rent for a fortnight, owing to a half-completed paint job. By six I was playing golf. I had intended to proceed more cautiously before resuming play—reread some long-forgotten instruction books, hit many dozens of practice shots—but the lure of the game in the green-and-gray city was overwhelming, and I made a dash for the links. I was well into my game before I realized that it was raining, that it had been raining all day, that the rain showed no signs of stopping, and that I did not know the whereabouts of my foul-weather gear or umbrella. No matter.

My impetuousness was not without limit. I held off playing the Old Course, the temple of golf, built on land that has served as golfing terrain since at least the fifteenth century, and instead played the New, laid out in 1895. Golf in a warm rain is one of life's more pleasant things, and it felt good to be playing again. I felt complete and total freedom, complete and total joy. It was the middle of summer and the only things in front of me were two months of golf and a man named Tom Watson, who was also going off the first tee of the New Course, by himself, in the warm rain. He invited me, a stranger, to join him.

Tom Watson was pulling his own trolley, playing yellow Top-Flites, using a Slazenger bag, a ten-finger baseball grip, laminated woods, a Ray Cook putter, and Ram irons, the Tom Watson Signature model. Tom Watson was a retired Edinburgh car mechanic who owned a cottage in St. Andrews. As we walked down the fairways he had me join him under his umbrella and we talked about Tom Watson, the golf professional.

"I guess you know that he's won the Open five times," I said. It's hard to tell a Scot a fact about golf that he does not know; Tom Watson knew that the other Tom Watson was the British Open champion in 1975, 1977, 1980, 1982, and 1983.

"One more, and he'll catch Harry Vardon," Tom Watson said. Harry Vardon, who won in 1896, 1898, 1899, 1903, 1911, and 1914, holds the record for most Open victories.

"Do you think he'll do it?" I asked.

"It's getting late in the day. His last best chance was here."

That was in 1984, when the Open was played over the Old Course for the twenty-third time. Watson shot a final-round 73, to Ballesteros's 69, and lost to the Spaniard by two shots. When the Open returned in 1990, both Ballesteros and Watson missed the cut.

"The Old Course has a tendency to bring out the best in a player's game, and the worst," Tom Watson said. "She's not meant for ordinary golf."

I told my partner about my lone bewildering game on the Old Course during a brief trip through St. Andrews six years earlier. One seemingly perfect drive finished in a bunker from which I had to play backwards; a pitch shot that landed a yard from the hole bounced over the green, down a hill, and disappeared into the gorse; a putt that I had expected to run downhill and break left-to-right proved to be uphill and right-to-left.

"Don't despair," Watson said. "She's not a love at first sight. The Old Course put your own Bobby Jones in quite a funk on his first visit."

I had heard that story. As a nineteen-year-old playing in the 1921 Open, Jones retired on the eleventh hole of his third round. He had had enough. When the Open next returned to the Old Course, in 1927, Jones won by six shots. Three years later, Jones won the British Amateur at St. Andrews, the first leg of his grand slam. In 1958, Jones was presented with the Freedom of the City, and in accepting the honor, he told the citizenry, who had packed into the Younger Graduation Hall, "I could take out of my life everything except my experiences at St. Andrews and I would still have had a rich and full life." If you want to know more about Jones and the Home of Golf, I recommend to you a book by Jones, *Golf Is My Game,* and particularly a chapter called "St. Andrews—A Short Love Story."

I asked Watson if there was any golfer today who was truly loved by the townspeople, as Jones was. "There is," he said.

"Who?" I asked. "Trevino?" Watson shook his head from east to west. "Ballesteros?" He continued to shake his head.

Watson? Palmer? Lyle? Faldo?

No, no, no, no.

Watson holed a putt on the sixth green, and I returned the heavy metal flagstick to the hole. I noticed that, despite the rain, the greens were practically dry.

"It's the Golden Bear, mon—Nicklaus," he said. "He's won us over."

St. Andreans have been warming up to Nicklaus for a while now, Watson explained. At first, they didn't understand his golf, so plodding, methodical, and systematic. But when he finished second in the 1964 Open on the Old Course, the townspeople acknowledged that he was an awesome talent. When the Open next came to the Old Course, in 1970, and Nicklaus won, they showed respect and admiration. When the Open returned to St. Andrews again in 1978, and Nicklaus won again, the townspeople decided that he had earned his place in the pantheon. But it was not until 1984 that they saw a side of Nicklaus they had not seen before, and that changed everything. Two days before the start of the 1984 Open, Nicklaus received an honorary Doctor of Laws degree from St. Andrews University. In accepting the honor, Nicklaus knelt before a vice chancellor of the university, a man named Watson. He was moved to tears. Townspeople who were there said that for one ephemeral and emotional moment they could feel the depth of Nicklaus's feelings for Scotland, St. Andrews, the Old Course, the Open championship, and the game itself.

I have wondered what kind of emotional toll the 1984 Open took on Tom Watson. That year he and Ballesteros were the two top players in the world, and they dominated the last round. Ballesteros, in the penultimate twosome, finished par, birdie, while Watson, in the final group, closed bogey, par, and those two shots were the difference. For Watson, the devastating shot was his second on the seventeenth, the Road Hole. (In Scotland, virtually every hole earns a name at some point in its life.) Watson played his fatal shot after a perfect drive: he tried to draw a 2-iron into a cross breeze, but he pushed the shot badly. It caught the breeze and went sailing. The ball bounced off the road that runs parallel to the hole and then off the wall, stopping practically against it. He made a bogey on seventeen when he needed a par, and made a par four on eighteen when he needed a two, and he has not been the same since. That is to say, he has not won any more major championships. People say that Watson's golfing problems since that 1984 Open have largely been about putting. Watson himself says that. Maybe. Ultimately, I think they're about having had a chance to win an Open on the Old Course, and not doing it.

If you look in nearly any book of golf records, you will see that the early Open championships were dominated by Tom Morris, Sr., known as Old Tom, and his son, Tom Morris, Jr., known as Young Tom. Old Tom won the Open in 1861, 1862, 1864, and 1867. Then came junior: Young Tom won in 1868, 1869, and

1870. No championship was played in 1871, but when the championship resumed in 1872 Young Tom won again. In Young Tom's middle two victories, his father placed second. Old Tom was born in St. Andrews and both men died there, and their names are still prominent in the town. There is a Tom Morris pro shop, owned now by Morris heirs, and a Tom Morris Drive in the newer part of town, up near the medical center, and the eighteenth hole of the Old Course is called Tom Morris. In the old cemetery, in the shadows of the cathedral ruins on the east side of town, there are many Morrises, including the tombstones of both Tom Morrises, which reveal that the elder Tom Morris lived a long time, from 1821 until 1908, while his son, Young Tom, was born in 1851 and died in 1875, at the age of twenty-four. In the history books in the St. Andrews library and on the postcards sold at the souvenir shops, you see dozens of pictures of both father and son: Old Tom is usually shown as a white-bearded octogenarian, bundled in woolen coats, with a cap pulled down far on his forehead, using a cane for support, and looking forlorn; Young Tom, clean-shaven except for a playful mustache, is usually captured with his coat unbuttoned, wearing a high-sitting tam-o'-shanter, and looking handsome and exuberant.

I set out to learn more about the Tom Morrises, and before long found myself sitting in the parlor room of an old St. Andrews farmhouse on the outskirts of town, surrounded by Morris memorabilia—capes and caps and clubs, scorecards and scrapbooks. The stuff belonged to a native St. Andrean, a wildly enthusiastic and energetic man named David Joy, whose shiny dark eyes had the disconcerting habit of flaring open without warning. Joy was an artist, engraver, actor, and golf history buff who played Old Tom Morris in an extemporaneous one-man play he performed from time to time. He spoke for hours and hours, telling me the great and sad story of the Tom Morrises. He stopped only for cigarettes and coffee.

On one of his trips to the kitchen, I sensed something peculiar was happening. Joy was gone for a long time, and I didn't hear any noises. I waited, but Joy never returned from that trip.

Something strange *had* happened. In Joy's place came Old

Tom Morris himself, wearing a long cape: *my host had assumed the persona of the senior Morris!* Joy's melodic Fife accent was gone, replaced with something harsher, more Germanic-sounding, and more difficult for me to understand. It was eerie and fascinating, and I paid close attention, of course, because, after all, how often does one get to visit with the ghost of Old Tom Morris? He sat right opposite me, in one of the parlor chairs, and he told me the story of his famous life, which I'll repeat here for you. I think Old Tom spoke to me because he wanted to get *his* version of his story *out.*

"Born in St. Andrews, I was, and took to the game as a boy of six. At eighteen I apprenticed to Mr. Allan Robertson, a ball-maker, and, before his end, a very fine club-maker. Can you read? Did you ever see his obituary in the *Citizen?* Let me find that obituary, where is it, where is it? Here. Good. Listen. 'He came of a golfing race.' Nothing truer has ever been written. His father was a ball-maker, and so was his father before him. And listen to this: 'It is a fact that his very few playthings as a child were golf clubs.' Aye, that was true for all of us. When you go to the cemetery next, you can see his tombstone just down from my own. I've not before nor since seen a grave marker quite like it: two crossed clubs and three featheries carved right into the stone. 'Twas the feathery that caused our falling out. The feathery, of course, was *the* ball until 1848, when the gutta-percha ball came about. A much better ball, the gutta-percha was, cheaper, went much farther. But Allan made his living by the feathery, and when he saw me once playing the gutty, he got hot and we went our ways.

"In '51, when I was thirty, I went to Prestwick, to be keeper of the green, and it was there and in that year that Thomas Junior was born. In '65, the Royal and Ancient urged me back to St. Andrews to be Custodian of the Links. I could still play in all the challenge matches I wanted, which was a significant income source for me, particularly when I took Tommy for a partner. I was a good striker of the ball, that is undeniable, but my putting was always too timid, I'll admit to that. Young Tom vowed early on to make up for my deficiencies in that area—he rolled the ball hard, and to the center of the hole. He'd say to me, 'The hole'll no' come to you.' His putting was legendary. He once had a round where he made ten putts of fifteen yards or more. Tommy had genius for the game. A child prodigy, he was. He was seventeen when he won the Open championship belt for the first time. He was twenty-one when he won it the fourth time. And twenty-four when he died.

"His death came on Christmas Day, 1875, three months after his wife, Margaret, and baby died in childbirth. They say he died a drunk, and that always hurts me, but you know the ways of a small town. I'll tell you what happened, but listen good, because I don't think I'll have the strength to tell it ever again.

"Our lives were good when, in September of 1875, Tommy and I went to North Berwick to play our old rivals, Willie Park, Sr., and his brother, Mungo. A challenge match, it was. While we were there, a telegraph came to the clubhouse: Margaret had gone into delivery and she and the baby were not well. A schooner was made available to us and we crossed the Firth of Forth, straight to St. Andrews, a grim and silent sailing. When we arrived at the harbor my brother met us with a small boat and the sad news. 'It's not true, it's not true,' Tommy kept shouting, but it was: Margaret and the baby had died. I knew he would never be the same after that. For weeks he did nothing. He was not a drinker at all, but he started drinking then, he did start then. He was interested in nothing. He played a match where he was four up with five holes to go, and he lost.

"Then Tommy was challenged by an amateur named Arthur Molesworth. The terms were harsh: twelve rounds over six days, starting on December first, with Young Tom giving Molesworth six shots a round. The weather turned icy cold, and the balls were frequently embedded in the snow. The greens had to be swept clear of the snow. The match continued on Molesworth's insistence, and Tommy won, but there was no joy in the thing.

"On Christmas Eve he had dinner with friends in Edinburgh.

He stayed out late, but in the morning I heard him move around. I waited for him to come down. He never did. When I went upstairs to look in on him, he was dead.

"Owing to the suddenness of his death, an autopsy was performed. The doctor said a blood vessel in the right lung had burst. I have always thought pneumonia was the root of it all, contracted during that six-day match in the bitter cold. The people in town said he died of a broken heart, but if it were as simple as that, then I would have died much earlier myself. Part of me did die on that Christmas Day. I turned over a corner of my room to Young Tom's memory. A shrine, it was, a shrine to everything he accomplished and everything he might've.

"Thirty-three years is a long time to outlive a son, too long. I was the grand old man of golf, and I had to live up to people's expectations of me. I was in demand to lay out new courses and make suggestions for old ones. I traveled all through Scotland, England, Wales, Ireland. Some of the courses I first routed are still famous today: Lahinch, Royal County Down, Dunbar, Carnoustie, Muirfield, nine holes at Dornoch, the New Course here.

"I was busy. I played in every Open right through '96, and served as the starter through '05. I made revisions on the Old Course, guarded her with all my energy. I was Custodian of the Links! Once, in '95, I felt the course was being abused, too much play, so I filled up the holes with dirt and closed her down. They had a fit, the town fathers did, that I would do such a thing without any 'authority.' But they kept the course closed for a week just the same. I *was* the authority, official or not. Once when I saw people playing on a Sunday, I opened up my window over my shop and shouted, 'If you gentlemen dinna need a rest on the Sawbath, the links does.'

"I don't fool myself, though. I might have been revered by the R. & A. members, in some manner—they commissioned my portrait and hung it in the Big Room—but those were different times. I was a servant to the club. When the new captain played himself in, I built his tee, and applauded the shot. I was one class and they were another. I didn't socialize with them. I answered their questions about the game. They took care of me in the monies. I had my own club, the New Club, where I was an honorary member. One day I fell down the steps there. People say I mistook the cellar door for the wine closet. Don't know why they say such things, don't know why. I was old, and I fell. Cracked my skull and died.

"On the day of my funeral, they closed down the links. I appreciated that, I did appreciate that. They buried me practically right next to Tommy. I appreciated that, too."

I needed—what do they call that?—a reality check. First, I had played golf with Tom Watson. All right, Tom Watson is a common name. Still, that was my first game since beginning the playing portion of my golfing adventure, and the name Tom Watson happens also to be the name of the seminal golfer of my early years in the game—a happy and unlikely coincidence. But to follow that with coffee with Old Tom Morris, and to hear him roar, "I was Custodian of the Links!"—*that* was too much. I called up the Management Committee of the St. Andrews Links Trust. I asked for the Custodian of the Links.

"We have no such position," I was told.

The title of the bossman, I learned, was "secretary." The secretary's name was Alec Beveridge. I made arrangements to see him.

"Does your job descend from the position of Custodian of the Links?" I asked.

"No," Beveridge said.

"Would you consider yourself a descendant of Old Tom Morris in any way?" I asked. I wanted to get to the bottom of things.

"No," Beveridge said.

He was a trim and fit man, with reddish hair, big reddish eyebrows, and a reddish tinge to his skin. He looked military. He wore a pale green business shirt, and his shave was absolutely perfect, even as midafternoon came and went. If he had told me that he had shaved at lunch, I would have believed him.

"But Old Tom was ultimately responsible for the running of the links, and so are you."

"Yes, but Old Tom was a beloved figure, and I am not."

"Oh," I said. Beveridge was candid, and credible. "Why is that?"

"It is a function of my job. An act of Parliament from 1974 obligates the Management Committee to administer the links with equal regard to all beneficiaries specified in the act: the members of the Royal and Ancient Golf Club, the citizens of St. Andrews, and all who resort here. The simple fact is that in summer, demand for play on the Old Course exceeds available playing time by a factor of five or six, and I know of no way to make everyone content. The interests of one group simply do not coincide with those of the others.

"Old Tom *was* the Old Course. If he felt a change needed to be made, he made it. Today, every golfer in the world thinks he owns the Old Course, and believes it is perfect exactly the way it is. Every man, woman, and child who comes here knows that the Old Course is a 'natural' course, and therefore nothing about it should be changed. But the fact is the course is always undergoing change, and always has, natural and by the hand of man. It breathes, it lives, it cannot remain static. I believe we must bring the St. Andrews links—the Old Course and the entire five-hundred-acre complex—into the twentieth century, and then get it ready for the twenty-first. For instance, I happen to think that in this day and age it is not unreasonable to have a car park for visiting golfers, or a place where they may change their clothes. I wanted to build a modest building for such a purpose, but there was an uproar. They called a special town meeting and three hundred people showed up. They said, 'We don't care how many Japanese die of pneumonia, we don't want your bloody changing room.' Every change is resisted, regardless of its merits. So Beveridge is not a popular chap."

It would be hard to imagine Old Tom getting worked up about changing rooms. He was a man who walked to the sea every morning, including the winter months, and went for a quick dip—three strokes out, three strokes in. It was his elixir. Then he'd walk across the first and last holes of the Old Course, dripping, and return to his flat above his shop.

"The Old Course is a phenomenon," Beveridge said. "The

New Course is a better course, per se, a better test of golf, but you cannot convince the people of that. It is simply not the Old Course. People have been conditioned by books and articles on the Open to think of the Old Course as truly the Home of Golf, as the course every golfer must play, as Mecca. They come here with this great feeling of anticipation, with this idea that they're going to savor their every shot, and document a goodly portion of their round on film or videotape. They must complete every hole, no matter what kind of score they run up, so they can have all the boxes in their scorecard filled up, so they can keep their scorecard. They'll say, 'I shot a hundred and thirteen on the Old Course, and I counted every last stroke.'

"The ultimate beauty of the Old Course is that it is not fair, and in that it approximates life. You can do all the planning you like, but in the end the Old Course has the final say. If you make a shot, you must accept the outcome. You can't play it again. That is preparation for life. On the Old Course, there are many shots, many bounces, that you may not like, that you may not think are fair, but you accept them, because you have no choice. You can plan only so much.

"Do you remember these wonderful lines from Robert Burns?

> *The best-laid schemes o' mice an' men*
> *Gang aft agley,*
> *An' lea'e us nought but grief an' pain*
> *For promised joy!*

"That is the Old Course. That was the Old Course a hundred years ago and that is the Old Course today. That is why you are here and why Old Tom Morris has not been lost to the winds of obscurity."

CHAPTER TWELVE

SWILCAN BURN

I HAD PLANNED TO PLAY the Old Course only once, on the last day of our two-week stay. St. Andrews has three other courses, and there are a dozen more within a fifteen-mile radius. I was playing every day and hitting balls every night. I wanted to wait as long as possible to play the Old Course, on the theory that each day would bring improvement and bring me a day closer to preparedness. And then early one morning, midway through the fortnight, the phone in our apartment rang. On the other end was Frank Cougan, the real-estate man through whom we were renting the flat.

"A fine and brilliant morning, it is," Frank said.

I had to take him at his word.

"I've secured a tee time on the Old for four P.M.—were you wanting a game?"

He caught me in a moment of weakness. I said yes.

"Good. Just make sure you're there well before four, because if they call your name and you're not there, you're out," Frank said.

Will do, I said.

"And do your warming up off on the side—they throw a fit if you take a lot of practice swings on the first tee," he said.

Right.

"And don't forget to bring your handicap certificate, or they won't let you off," he said.

Check.

"Now, if you want a caddie, you should secure one now, otherwise there'll be none around this afternoon."

Good idea, I said.

"And bring plenty of balls," he said.

"Will two dozen be enough?" I asked.

"That should be fine." I was not encouraged.

"Is there anything else I should know about?"

"Naw, that's all, my friend—the important thing is to enjoy it."

As soon as I hung up the phone, I started growing nervous. I swallowed a bowl of cereal and walked down to the Old Course, to secure a caddie; I was eager to make the round a success.

It was still early when I arrived. The sea was calm and the clubhouse of the Royal and Ancient Golf Club was dark and shut. There were at least a dozen caddies lingering about, mostly young men wearing windbreakers, rubbing their hands in the morning chill. I saw a caddie I knew from the tour named Neil, who had worked for a French player, Emmanuel Dussart. But when Dussart hit a dry patch, Neil, a fleshy-faced bespectacled twenty-year-old, ran out of money and went home, to St. Andrews. I wanted to say hello, but didn't. It seemed not right for me to be on a golfing holiday while he was looking for work. Suddenly, hiring a caddie seemed pretentious and unnecessary, and I decided I'd take my chances and go it alone. When I saw Neil heading off the first tee, bag on shoulder, I was relieved.

It was a spectacular morning, and I was happy to hang out. The first tee of the Old Course is like no other spot in golf. From it you see the wide stretch of beach used in the opening scene of *Chariots of Fire.* You see the glistening bay. You see the clubhouse of the R. & A. You see Tom Morris's shop. You hear English in every imaginable accent and several foreign languages, too. You might well see a golfing celebrity. Earlier that morning, Sean Connery, the Scottish-born actor who is an expert golfer, had been spotted. I saw Michael Bonallack, the secretary of the R. & A., the man who runs the Open and one of golf's most accomplished amateurs. And I thought I saw Tip Anderson, Arnold Palmer's exclusive, and famous, British caddie.

Tip Anderson's Open record was a matter of caddie history. In 1960, Palmer, with Anderson on the bag, finished second in the Open, held that year in St. Andrews, the town of Tip's birth. The next year, at Royal Birkdale, Palmer won the Open, with Anderson caddying. In the following year, when the Open was at Royal Troon, Palmer, with Anderson, won again. In 1964 the Open returned to St. Andrews but Palmer did not come over. Even though he had won the Masters three months earlier he felt he was not playing well enough to win, and that was enough to keep him at home. Palmer recommended Tip to Tony Lema, and Tip led Tony to victory. If a World Caddie Hall of Fame is ever established, Tip, I'm sure, will be an inaugural inductee. I asked a caddie if that man on a distant bench was Mr. Tip Anderson.

"Are ya needin' a caddie?" I was asked in return.

No, I said, just curious to know if I was looking at Tip.

"If you're wanting to meet Tip Anderson, try around noon," I was told.

"Around noon? Isn't he on the golf course by noon?"

"You dinna look fer him here."

"Where do you look for him?" I asked.

"The Crit, more than likely," the caddie said, and he wandered off.

Having nothing more urgent to do, I decided to seek out Tip Anderson. At noon I went to the Criterion Bar, on South Street. The barmaid there told me to try the Cross Keys Bar, on Market Street. And there, at a corner table, sitting with an elderly woman and a younger man, was the legendary caddie.

As soon as I saw Anderson, I realized that beyond a few slim and obvious facts, I knew very little about him: I had no idea what he was *like.* When Tip went to the bar—a half-pint of lager and a dram of whisky for the woman, pints of lager for himself and the other man—I got a good look at him. He was about six feet tall and rail-thin; he could not have weighed more than one hundred and forty pounds. I had never before seen a caddie with skin like his, so milky and smooth, with no lines at all, even though he was approaching sixty. He wore Foot-Joy sneakers; thin plaid pants; a white golf shirt; a pale blue Old Course cap from which his white sideburns tumbled out; and an expensive Sunderland rain jacket. He wore a pin on his left collar, a tiny multicolored umbrella, which is Arnold Palmer's corporate logotype. He didn't look much different from the old pictures I had remembered of him. The barman took Tip's money and said, "James, Jimmy, Jim, Jim, Jim." As Tip returned to his table, I realized that until then I had not even known his real name.

Outside the bar, it was a bright and shiny day; the streets were filled with shoppers and tourists, and the links were crowded with golfers. But the Cross Keys was dim and smoky, immune from hubbub. For the most part, its patrons sat silently and drank darkly.

When I had entered the bar, I passed at the door a bearded man wearing a three-piece suit and a tartan tie who played harmonica with a plastic cup at his feet. Sometime later, he came into the bar, ordered a pint, paid with an assortment of small coins, and sat at a table, near two women. They were visitors to St. Andrews, tourists. I don't know if they were looking for local color, but they were about to find it. The man began to raise his voice incoherently and started tugging clumsily at the belt of his suit pants. I thought he was going to disrobe. Tip, whose table was twenty feet away from this activity, stood straight up, walked over to the man and instructed him to behave himself. The women gathered their shopping bags and left. The man stared at the floor and Tip returned to his seat. Nobody else batted an eye.

In time, I introduced myself to Tip and asked if I might sit down with him, and he said sure. The other man was named Jack, and as best I could tell he had worked as a caddie on the

Old Course during Tip's heyday, in the sixties. Then Jack had been a student studying zoology at the university; now he was a lecturer in computers. I never learned the name of the elderly woman. She had a severe Scottish brogue and I could not understand what little she said.

"This man was the best," Jack said to me, hoisting his glass in Tip's direction. "The caddies you see on the tour today, they're just bag-carriers. Tip knew how to put a club in his man's hands."

"I was the best," Tip said. The old woman nodded, left and right and up and down. I did not know if she was in agreement or disagreement or what.

"They don't know today what it means to know a course," Jack said. "This man knew every blade of grass on the Old Course. He knew every distance, not with some yardage book, but with his eyes."

"Knew every blade of grass, I did," Tip said.

"And the break of every putt," Jack said.

"Every last putt," Tip said.

Jack continued in praise of Tip for a while, and then the two launched into a discussion of a St. Andrews caddie who had recently died, at the age of forty-seven. Jack became very sad. Tip took off his hat and sang an old Scottish dirge, which moved Jack nearly to tears. Tip sang loudly, and with a good, clear voice, but nobody beyond our table looked at him.

When he was through, Tip sensed the awkward sobriety that had overcome his table. He changed tempo. He put his nose about six inches away from mine and sang "Mr. Sandman."

"Hey, Mr. Sandman, bring me a dream. . . ."

He was staring me right in the eye, and I had no choice but to stare back. I kept smiling, because I didn't know what else to do.

"Make her the cutest thing I've ever seen. . . ."

When he was through, Jack said, "You could have been a great crooner, James."

"Could have been," Tip said. There was a moment of silence for what could have been.

I asked Tip if he was caddying much these days.

"I went down this morning, 'round ten, but there were too many in front of me, so I took my name off the list," he said.

Jack said, "Can you believe they make him wait in the queue, just like everybody else? Can you believe that?"

I felt I should be agreeable; I said I could not believe that. I asked Tip if his father had been a caddie, too.

"Caddied the Old Course for forty years," Tip said.

"Long time," I said. "Did your father ever meet Old Tom Morris?" Tip was born in 1932, and Morris died in 1908, so that seemed to me entirely possible.

"Good God, woman, how old do you think I am?" Tip said. His locution puzzled me, disturbed me, but I was a guest at his table so I said nothing. Soon after, Jack and Tip left the Cross Keys for the Crit. I was not disappointed.

"Mr. Palmer is a great man," Tip said before he left. "He's never treated me like a caddie. Whenever there's somebody important around, he introduces me. He says, 'Do you know Tip Anderson?' "

I'm not sure what prompted Tip to tell me that. Maybe he thought that that was what I had come to hear.

In the main, St. Andrews is a thinking person's town; the townspeople have an intelligence that you simply don't encounter every day. In my effort to get to know the place, I talked at length with about two dozen people, both in formal interviews and in unexpected encounters, and again and again I heard thoughts that were unique, insightful, and interesting.

I met a man named Craig Nisbet, a reporter on the *St. Andrews Citizen,* who told me about the relationship between the locals and the visitors. "Consider the Old Course caddies," he said. "A lot of people come here and they say, 'Those caddies—what characters!' Of course, a lot of these guys are out of their regular work, and that's why they're caddying. They'd rather carry two bags, but the authorities are trying to spread the work around so they're allowed to carry only one. They may not be happy, but they'll take you around the course just the same, tell you the name of every bunker, if you like."

I met a man named Bobby Burnet, a retired schoolteacher who is the historian to the Royal and Ancient Golf Club, and I asked him about the claim that golf was not truly Scottish in origin but that it had evolved from a Dutch game. Burnet answered, "Whenever you hear someone mention a supposed ancestral form of golf, ask if the game had a hole. That is the distinguishing characteristic of golf: you start in a specified spot, and you proceed to hit your ball until you knock it into a hole. Without the hole, you don't have golf. I know of no other game where that is the object."

I met an eighty-eight-year-old man named John Gilchrist, a Classics scholar, a former provost of St. Andrews, and a former playing partner, as a university student, of Laurie Auchterlonie, winner of the 1902 U. S. Open. He explained to me why one seldom hears a Scot bragging about a round of golf: "The Scot comes in from his best-ever round. The man on the veranda says to him, 'Well, how'd you go today?' He answers, 'Not bad.' We fear that boastfulness can anger the gods. We're very much like the ancient Greeks in that regard."

I met a Japanese academic named Yasuo Asakura who told me that many of his countrymen deserved their reputation for slow play in St. Andrews and explained the root of it. "For many Japanese who come here, this is the first golf they have ever played on a real course, and they don't know how to go about it," he said. "In Japan, most golfers play only on the driving range. The club is unaffordable. We come here for affordable golf."

I met a St. Andrews police sergeant named Malcolm Stewart, a five-handicap golfer, who explained to me that there were people who would commit all types of crimes—tax evasion, golf-club theft, armed robbery—who would never cheat in golf. "When you cheat in golf, you see, the only person you are cheating is yourself," he said. "And there's no pleasure in that, no benefit in it at all."

I met a former captain of the Royal & Ancient, J. Stewart Lawson, who also belongs to three American clubs—Pine Valley,

Augusta National, and the Los Angeles Country Club. He explained to me how Britons and Americans reveal their fundamental philosophical differences through golf. "Americans are success oriented, and they want to finish their round with a score. The British are enjoyment oriented, and want to have a good, close match. Ultimately, these attitudes come from the marketplace. In America, you can get kicked out of a job. In Britain, it's awfully hard to get sacked."

In St. Andrews, a city of pubs and churches and students and golfers, there were interesting ideas lurking all over.

"Move it, people, for crying out loud!" It was four P.M. and Frank Cougan, my real-estate man and golf partner, was on the first tee. There is a public road that crosses the first and eighteenth fairways of the Old Course, and it was sprinkled with tourists who strolled merrily and obliviously as Frank prepared to tee off. He did not expect to clear away everybody, for the Old Course is literally a public playing field, bordered by a beach, a museum, and a pedestrian street.

Frank managed to scare off nearly everybody in front of us, but there was nothing that he or anyone else could do about the human masses at our backs. The first tee attracts all manner of casual onlookers. Typically, they have no vested interest in your affairs, but if they're around when you stick your tee in the ground and your ball on the tee, they're going to stay around to analyze your swing and to bear witness to the outcome of your opening shot. I felt that if I could just get off the first tee acceptably, everything else would follow. Frank and I were joined by a muscular man named John, who carried a huge, cumbersome golf bag, the kind normally reserved for the back end of a motorized cart, the usual mode of transportation over John's home course in Miami.

The first hole, called Burn, is a par-four of 370 yards and it was playing downbreeze. The first fairway is essentially unmissable. There is nothing—no bunkers, gorse, whin, heather, bracken, or rough—to impede you. The first fairway is massive and wholly inviting. The only thing you must avoid is a wicked slice, because the beach, off to the right, is out of bounds. For reasons not clear to me now, I hit a 3-iron on the first hole, and I hit it well. Striking the ball was a total physical pleasure, and the ball flew, bounced, and rolled some 220 yards. When you hit a golf ball squarely, you have the sensation that you have made contact with absolutely nothing: you just hear a firm *click* and watch the ball sail. What a delight.

Frank and John used drivers, and got off the tee ably: my shot finished about ten yards behind Frank's; John's drive, a pop-up, finished about ten yards behind mine. A good start for all of us.

"Did you enjoy that, Michael?" Frank asked as we walked off the tee.

"I certainly did," I said. Immediately, I wondered if the best round of my life was in store for me that day. All the conditions seemed optimal: the congenial company, the wonderful weather, the historic venue.

I asked Frank, who knew the Old Course intimately, for the distance of my second shot.

He answered without hesitation. "One-fifty to the hole, one-twenty-five to carry the burn. It'll play one-fifteen over the burn, with the breeze." The first hole got its name for the brook, or burn, that runs in front of its green.

There are many books that explain how to play the Old Course and each tells you that the second shot on the first hole plays longer than it measures. If I had hired a caddie, I'm sure he would have told me the same thing. (He would also have told me to hit a driver off the first.) My full pitching wedge shot normally flies one hundred and twenty yards in still, warm conditions. I was thinking in terms of perfection. I figured a full wedge would get me just over the burn and my ball would then roll to the hole on the firm, running greens. I hit the wedge about as well as I could, and with the shot at its apex I heard Frank cheerfully say, "Lovely," and then I saw the ball land smack in the Swilcan Burn. I took my penalty (third shot), pitched on (fourth), and three-putted (strokes five, six, and seven) for a triple-bogey start. My perfect round was not to be.

I was having one miserable hole after another. Bogeys were bright spots. My slogging play did nothing to diminish Frank's enthusiasm, and it seemed to positively lift John, who was having the game of his life. The Old Course, the strange beast, was bringing out the best in John's game. He was following good shots with excellent shots—an inspired round. Frank was on his game, making par after par after par, enjoying his role as tour guide to two Americans. He was a wonderful host; he showed us all the sights. On the fourteenth, the Long Hole, he said, "This is Hell Bunker," and John said, "Most famous bunker in golf." On the seventeenth, Frank said, "This is the Road Hole," and John said, "Most famous hole in golf." On the eighteenth, Frank said, "This is the Swilcan Burn Bridge," and John said, "The most famous bridge in golf." My only thought was that the damn thing wasn't high enough to make jumping off worthwhile.

CHAPTER THIRTEEN

R. FORGAN

NINETY-FIVE WHACKS. It was embarrassing. In a week I would be leaving St. Andrews and I was determined to have a better go over the Old Course in my second and last try. I needed Stark. I called him and asked if I could come over and see him—he was an hour and a half away by car—and he, no doubt having detected the urgency in my voice, said, "Come over, come over at once."

We settled in our chairs. Stark was wearing his white loafers. The shop assistant brought in coffee and Stark stirred his with the letter opener. (The man's life plainly had patterns.) He asked, "Are you enjoying St. Andrews?" He slowly peeled the plastic wrapper off his cigar. He seemed never to be in a rush.

"I am," I said, temporarily expunging from memory my game with Frank and John.

"Have you noticed that wherever you go in St. Andrews you can hear the sea gulls?" I hadn't noticed that. "Pay attention to that in the future, Michael, throughout Scotland. When you're getting near the linksland you'll hear the sea gulls first." He lit the cigar.

"And what do you think of my country so far?" Stark, like

most Scots, was a nationalist, and eager to remind you that Scotland is a country unto itself.

"I like it," I said. "I feel at home here."

"There is nothing like Philadelphia or New York or London in Scotland," Stark said. "Our scale is small. There's a sense in some places—in England, in America—that smallness is something you put up with while you wait for bigger things. That is not our way."

You could sense that in St. Andrews, that the small town—where the dangerous whispering of neighbors is offset by the well-rooted reliability of friends; where boredom is relieved on the golf courses and in the pubs—was central to the Scottish way of life.

"Now tell me about the state of your game," Stark said. "But before you do, remember that the state of one's game is ever-evolving. In my experience, one's golf is never as good as one thinks it is, but never as bad, either."

I told Stark about my re-entry into golf as a player. I described to him a round I had played on the Balcomie Golf Course, home of the Crail Golfing Society. The course, about ten miles from St. Andrews and routed by Old Tom on a little peninsula sticking out into the Firth of Forth, measured only 5,720 yards from the back tees (the Old Course is 6,604 from the middle tees) and par was only 69 (the Old Course is a 72). But it was a wonderful and interesting track regardless of its numbers and it had, like the Old Course, a burn on the first and a long par-four seventeenth known as the Road Hole. My play was dull going out, ten over the front-nine par of 36, but improved radically coming in. I birdied the seventeenth (a big drive followed by a bouncing 3-iron that stopped six feet from the hole) which brought me to level par through the first eight holes of the back nine, ten over for the day. As I stood on the tee of the long uphill par-three finishing hole, I knew I had a chance to make a little personal history, golf division. If I finished with a three, I would, for the first time in my life, have a nine-hole score of even par and a total under eighty for the first time since the summer after my senior year of high school. I made a six. A triple bogey. A disaster.

The next day I played, if that's the right verb, the Old Course. And the day after that I was in Stark's office.

"You have a dangerous mind, Michael," Stark said. "Hypnosis may be what you need."

"All through the back nine, until the eighteenth, I had this recurring feeling that my real game was ready to break loose, that just being in Scotland was bringing out the best in my golf."

"It has for others," Stark said.

"Like Tom Weiskopf," I said.

"Aye. A brilliant player, he was, but a problem with the head—the temper, the temper. All that talent, but just the one major—the Open at Troon, 1973. Have you caddied for him?"

"No, but I've interviewed him."

"And what did you learn?"

"He said he knew from the first time he ever came to Scotland that he would someday win an Open here, for two reasons. First, because he loved the country; he said being in Scotland made him try hard, because he wanted to show the Scots the kind of shots he could play. And second, because he *liked* the weird bounces, good and bad, you get on the Scottish links courses like Troon. He said when he played in the major tournaments in the United States, and the conditions were perfect, he expected himself to play perfect golf. And when he didn't, he'd go crazy."

"Lose the head," Stark said.

"Right. At Troon, he hit perfect shots that took bad bounces and finished poorly, and he hit poor shots that took good bounces and finished well. He said he felt no inner turmoil for the entire week. He'd play the shot, and however it came out, he accepted it. He said Scotland brought that out in him. He said, 'It's too bad I was born in the United States—I should have been born a Scot.' "

"Then we may never have heard of him," Stark said.

"Why's that?"

"His whole technique might have been different."

And with that Stark stood up and went head first into a cluttered office closet and emerged with a hickory-shafted mashie, a dozen loose balls that looked as if they had been made by Old Tom himself, and two tubes of modern balls. "Now, let's see what you're doing," he said.

We worked our way over to the practice field of the Crieff Golf Club. Stark handed me the old club. It had a richly colored brown shaft, a thin grip wrapped with a thin strip of hardened black leather, and a shiny forged head with worn scoring lines. The back was stamped with the name of its maker, *R. Forgan, St. Andrews.* Stark reached into the pocket of his windbreaker and dropped one of the dozen loose balls at my feet. I picked it up. It was gray, mealy, and small. The dimples were shallow. I could just make out the brand name: *Price's Everlasting.*

"Here is some equipment from long before your time, long before my own," Stark said. "I want you to see how difficult the game used to be."

The day was gray and cold and blowy and the practice grounds, off in a field far from the clubhouse, were empty and dark. I took some practice swings with the old mashie but the grip was slippery and I felt myself holding onto the club hard, to prevent it from flying away.

"Gentle, Michael, gentle. In golf you must always be gentle. Give a good spit into your hands, 'twas the early golf glove," Stark said. I spat and rubbed my hands until they were sticky.

"Now as you swing the club, feel the weight of the clubhead, up through the soft wood of the shaft, through the grip, into your hands, and throughout your body. Become aware of the feel of the clubhead. You can feel it more with that old hickory-shafted mashie than your modern clubs." I continued taking practice swings, and I started to feel the clubhead, and also the softness of the shaft. It was more malleable than any club I had ever swung. I could sense the care and skill that went into the making of the club. I was aware of the club's *life.* I could feel the mass of the clubhead causing the shaft to bend, and that was a unique sensation for me. My own clubs have stiff shafts and my unfortunate, largely uncontrollable, lifelong tendency has been to try to swing with all my available might. People have been telling me for years to slow down, but knowing what you need to do and doing it are not the same thing. I made some practice swings that felt good, but I did not delude myself. Swinging at daisies is like playing electric guitar with a tennis racket; if it were that easy we could all be Jerry Garcia. The ball changes everything. When Stark told me to give the Price's Everlasting a try, I felt myself grow tight. It was time to plug in.

I took a deep breath—an anxiety antidote prescribed by my late high school golf coach fifteen years earlier—and I swung fluidly and I caught the ball cleanly and well. The ball did not come off the mashie club face with the zip or pep that it would have off a modern 5-iron. Its flight had a floating quality and the ball landed about one hundred and twenty-five yards away. (A 5-iron might have gone one hundred and seventy.)

"Not bad," Stark said. "Try it again." He put another old ball in front of me. "On you go," he said.

An ugly impulse inside me took over. In trying to hit the second ball farther than the first, I swung harder. I hit it the same distance, but thirty yards to the left of the other ball. Stark said nothing, but I knew what he was thinking: I had missed the whole point. With the soft-shafted mashie and the old, soft ball there was no need for forcefulness: the combination of ball and club was incapable of producing big hits anyway. Stark made no comment. He just dropped another one and said, "On you go." I pulled another shot. He dropped another, I pulled another. He dropped another, I pulled another. This went on for a while.

The setting was out of a dream: I was swinging a beautiful hand-crafted mashie and launching shots into the Scottish wind under the careful eye of a master teacher and to the accompaniment of his reassuring burr. But in golf the pull of one's historic tendencies is terribly strong, and every time I completed a backswing I became overwhelmed with my usual irresistible urge, to hit the ball hard. We switched to a modern 5-iron and modern balls and the results were the same: basically good contact, but shots that sailed far off the intended line, most often to the left, occasionally to the right.

"There's nothing terribly wrong with your mechanics," Stark said finally. "But your swing is horrendous." I felt as if I were standing before a judge, and in a sense I was. "Your problems are all about tempo, about timing. In order to *feel* the proper tempo of a swing, you have to *hear* the swing. You have to make the *sounds* that accompany a good shot in order to make a good shot."

Stark took my 5-iron from me and hit a ball. He had a small hip turn and, despite a big shoulder turn, he didn't take the club back very far at all. He gripped the club as if he were holding the mushy arm of a tiny infant. There was nothing fast about his swing; the clubhead was never a blur. On his downswing, all the moving parts came together at once, not in pieces. The first ball he hit, without a single practice swing, shot off like a rocket, curving gently from right to left and landing ten feet to the right of the stake for which he was aiming.

"*Hear* the sound the shaft makes as it comes through the air, *listen* to how rhythmic and sweet that sound is. Hear the sound of the clubhead making good contact with the ball, and then, right afterward, the ground. These are the lovely sounds of good golf, as lovely as the ovation for the Open champion, as lovely as the sound of a dropping putt, as lovely as the singing of chirping birds." Stark was a poet.

"Listen to these three swings," he continued. He made a slow rhythmic swing and the shaft made a soft, low, consistent *schwoo* sound as it resisted the air. "That was Lyle," he said. He made a second, slightly faster swing, which produced a more high-pitched but still consistent *schwoo.* "That was Faldo." Then Stark made a fast, energetic swing that produced a high-pitched but even *schwoo.* "That was Olazábal," he said.

"There's no one proper sound. The only requirement is that the sound be pleasing."

Stark made another swing, and I closed my eyes and listened for the sounds of good golf. I heard them. They *were* lovely sounds. When I opened my eyes, I looked out to the stake and saw his ball fall right near it again. He handed the club back to me. "Try to make nice sounds," he said. "On you go."

It had been years since I had heard a swing thought that was completely new to me, and I found it immediately effective. I alternated between the hickory-shafted club and my own graphite-shafted club. It was easier to make a pleasant, even sound with the whippier hickory club; R. Forgan of St. Andrews seemed to have built a rhythm right into the club. But I found myself swinging rhythmically with my own club, too. By concentrating only on the sound, I lost the irresistible urge to hit the ball hard. My downswing was smoother, less rushed. I had more time to get my legs, hips, shoulders, arms, and hands synchronized in the manner necessary to hit a golf ball well. I remember the pleasure I felt then, the intellectual and sensory pleasure of being totally consumed in my effort to hit good golf shots.

Stark went back to the shop, and left me with the balls and the clubs and the use of his practice field, and I stayed there for hours. Scottish golfers, in general, both professional and amateur, do not share the fascination for the driving range that American and Japanese golfers do (there are fewer than a dozen driving ranges in Scotland). For most of the afternoon I was out there alone. But then a boy, not yet a teenager, came out to hit balls, making one good shot after another. I tried to be inconspicuous, but I could not stop staring at him, I could not stop listening to him. Even though he was a skinny kid, the kind who typically tries to wallop the ball with everything he has to keep up with his older sister, there was none of that in this boy's swing. Finally, I asked if he minded if I watched, and listened. I stood behind him and could hear his gentle inhaling on his backswing and exhaling on his downswing. The shaft of his club cutting through the air sounded just like Stark's re-creation of Sandy Lyle. I went back to my ball and tried those very things: inhaling on the backswing, exhaling on the downswing, hearing the sounds of a fluid swing (thoughts I have since seen explored in an interesting book called *Quantum Golf* by a Swedish golf teacher, Kjell Enhager). I started making good swings, and I became entranced by what I was doing. Everything felt good. I walked to the pro shop, thanked my teacher, and returned to St. Andrews. I could not wait to return to the first tee of the Old Course.

CHAPTER FOURTEEN

ELYSIAN FIELDS

I HAVE IN FRONT OF ME the golf ball I used in my second and last game over the Old Course. That is to say, I needed only one ball for the entire eighteen holes: nothing out of bounds, nothing in the burn, nothing in the gorse, nothing, as the old-time caddies say, unrecoverable. The ball is a balata-covered 100-compression Titleist, the Tour 100 model, stamped with a 1, that I bought, enticed by its shininess, in a St. Andrews golf shop for seventy-five pence, picked out of a barrel labeled American Lake Balls. Now, eighteen holes later, it has a faint scrape mark on one side and a slight cut filled with a grass stain on the other, and it is scarred throughout by tiny pockmarks caused by sitting under water for too long a time. I wish I could find out what other strange things happened to the ball during its submerged life. Somehow, somewhere the ball acquired special powers. I have considered breaking it out for an important match, but I don't think I will; if I were to lose it I would be very glum, for it is the most tangible link I have to my last game at St. Andrews. I know I wrote early on that I am not the sort to trap you in the cafeteria and recount, blow by blow, an entire round, and I stand by that, but I ask for your indulgence here. We are, after all, talking about the Old Course.

Maybe you have heard horror stories about how difficult it

is to get a tee time on the Old Course in summer, and it is, unless you are, as I was, a singleton. A player by himself may ask to join any threesome. I arrived at ten minutes to five on Monday, August fifth, and at exactly five o'clock—with sunset still nearly five hours away—I teed off. I played with men named George Craig, a smallish, balding retired Edinburgh gardener with powerful arms and a flat stomach; William Herd, a gigantic, long-whacking two-handicapper who ran a bar in Leith, outside Edinburgh; and Paul Hackland, a red-haired boyish-looking man who was the steward of the New Club, the place where Old Tom had his fatal fall. The Scots are a wonderfully friendly people, and George, William, and Paul didn't seem to mind having me at all. When I asked if my camera-carrying, wildflower-collecting, linksland-enjoying wife could walk with us, they perked right up; unlike most male American golfers, male Scottish golfers celebrate female interest in the game. They remember that Mary, Queen of Scots, was a golf buff. At the Old Course, and throughout Scotland, non-playing spouses (these days, typically women, but that will change) are welcome to walk the links. (American resort owners who charge a "walking fee" or a "riding fee" would be appalled to see that most Scottish courses also welcome dog-walkers, runners, fishermen, photographers, naturalists, ornithologists, picnickers, artists, kite-fliers, and other romantics.) I know the precise time of my opening blow because Christine took a wonderful photograph of it, with my partners on the left, me in follow-through staring down the shot on the right, two dozen passers-by looking on behind us, and behind them the R. & A. fortress with the long gold hand of its exterior clock pointing straight up, the small hand at the V.

As in my first shot in my first game on the Old Course, I used a 3-iron again. Stupid, perhaps, but at the time I had my reasons: there was a fresh draft blowing down-hole, the tee markers were well forward, and the only thing I *had* to do was avoid a just-out-of-the-car slice. I hit the 3-iron horribly, thin and off the heel, and it bounced straight down the fairway for about one hundred and fifty yards. That was the last abominable shot I hit that day.

The root of my opening-shot problem was obvious: I had

rushed. As I walked off the first tee, I remembered my new mantras—to inhale on the backswing, exhale on the downswing, and to create the sounds of good golf. If my playing partners figured me for a total dud after my initial shot, I changed their minds with my second, a cracking 3-iron from about one hundred and ninety yards, right over the burn and onto the green. Three putts later I had an opening bogey five, and even though I should have had a par, I wasn't displeased. I tried to be like Peter on the thirty-third hole of the Portuguese Open. He didn't think about how his quadruple bogey there had wiped his name off the leader board. He thought instead of how lucky he was that a caddie had found his ball, for without that discovery his eight might have been a ten and he might have missed the cut. I could have been disappointed that my lag putt from thirty-five feet went no closer than four feet, and that my four-footer caught a lip and stayed out, and that I opened with a bogey instead of a par. But on the other hand, after my first shot I could have easily hacked a few more, maybe dunked a ball in the burn again, and ended up with another seven. Bogey five wasn't bad at all, I reasoned. I kept that attitude throughout the round, which I now consider to be among the most memorable and fun I have ever played.

Beyond its antiquity, it is hard to say precisely what makes the Old Course such a pleasure. Part of the aura lies in its being so close to the sea. The air smells good. The setting is literally bucolic. On the way out, you are vaguely mindful that you are playing away from town, and on the way in you are keenly aware of returning to civilization; you see church steeples, hotels, pedestrians, cars. There is a *Canterbury Tales* quality to a game on the Old Course. Your round is a strange and long trip and you have no idea who or what you will encounter, or where you will stop. In Mrs. Kruger (a bunker on the ninth)? On Ginger Beer (the fourth hole)? In the Valley of Sin (a depression in front of the eighteenth green)?

Maybe the best thing about the Old Course, once you come to know and understand its quirks, is that it demands your total involvement. The ideal line off the tee is seldom obvious. Nearly every approach shot requires you to consider a chain of humps and hollows in deciding how to get your ball headed hole-bound. Putts are a total mystery. I four-putted the third green for a double-bogey six, but I had rolled each putt on my intended line. In other words, my stroke was OK, but my judgment was inexplicably bad. And yet, despite my inept green reading, I could feel myself concentrating, I could feel myself employing my new swing thoughts, I could feel my involvement. I was lost in the game.

I went out in 45, with twenty-two putts, which is terrible putting, even allowing for the huge and deceptive Old Course greens. When, at the turn, I realized that the wind had been helping on the first seven holes, I had no choice but to regard my 45 as a poor score. I wasn't displeased with my play, just my score; I had blown the downbreeze opportunity. The hard stuff was to come: holes twelve through eighteen would be played into a wicked quartering wind. And yet I wasn't worried about them. I wasn't worried about anything. That was a function of my total involvement.

I made a par on the tenth, a par-four of only 318 yards. I made a par on the 172-yard eleventh, one of the two par-threes on the Old Course, and was pleased to do that, for the eleventh, where Bobby Jones made his exit, has a weird green that slopes severely from the back to the front. The pin was in the middle and my tee shot finished above the hole; I did well to two-putt.

Then on the twelfth, a 316-yard par-four, I had a bit of luck. I didn't remember the hole well, so I hit a 3-iron to be safe, and when I walked to my ball I saw what you cannot see from the tee: a congregation of four menacing fairway bunkers beginning about 200 yards from the tee. I was ten yards short of the first one—lucky.

The green on the twelfth has two very definite tiers and the pin was on the upper one. I punched a 9-iron and my ball finished about twenty feet from the hole. I made the putt for a birdie, the longest putt I had made in two weeks of golf. On the thirteenth, a 398-yard par-four from the middle tee (and 425 from the championship tee), I made another par. I was in what the pros used to call "the zone."

Then came the fourteenth, the Long Hole, one of the two

par-fives on the Old Course, a 523-yard fascination. You can't go right, or you'll be out of bounds. You can't go left, or you'll be in the Beardies, an assemblage of five deep, mean bunkers. But if you drive your golf ball well you have the privilege of finding a much-sought and largely elusive piece of golf terrain: St. Andreans call it the Elysian Fields. As I stood on the tee, I felt a terrific calm, but a controlled excitement, too. I exhaled all my air. I thought about the sounds of golf. I looked right at the numeral 1 on my Titleist. I went into my backswing and inhaled. I shifted gears and left my backswing for my downswing, exhaling and hearing a melodic, even *schwoo.* I drove the ball as far and as straight as any ball I have ever hit in my life. It went about 260 yards, into the wind.

William drove his out with me. I stood next to him as he ripped his second shot over the massive and dangerous Hell Bunker. I was thinking about playing short of Hell, leaving a shot to the green of one hundred and twenty yards or so. William sensed my internal debate and said, "Go for it." I hit a four-wood just like the drive, same swing, same piercing flight. I had never before hit such powerful shots back-to-back. The second shot finished thirty-five yards short of the green.

The ground in front of the fourteenth green was firm and the grass was closely cropped, so I tried the local shot. I putted (in a former life the sand wedge would have come out automatically). The ball skimmed over the fairway and rolled on to the green true and well and finished ten inches from the cup. William knocked the ball back to me, and for a moment I was upset: I had wanted to *hole* that tiny birdie putt. But I didn't let the thought linger.

The only match I was playing was an internal one, and I felt it to be as exciting as any golf competition I had ever witnessed, as a spectator, reporter, caddie, or player. I had just made a birdie on the Long Hole, one of the sternest holes in all of golfdom, to go two under on the back nine of the Old Course as it played into the wind. I realized I was only seven over par for the day, and I thought, *If I can play the remaining holes in even par, I'll break eighty!*

A damning thought.

On fifteen, I knocked my drive into Sutherland, a pot bunker from which I needed two swipes just to get out, and made a double-bogey six. Then I three-putted the sixteenth for a bogey. My round was unraveling.

I was determined to play the Road Hole well. I aimed my drive out of bounds and tried to play a draw, the classical approach to the hole. But I got nervous during my downswing and yanked my arms across my body and pulled the ball wildly, into something resembling a Kansan hayfield. I searched and searched for the American Lake Ball and was growing despondent over the possibility of losing it and either having to go back to the tee to play another, as the rules require, or not having a legal score. And then Paul, my partner, found the ball. It was gnarled in grass, but it was mine. I knocked it forward, but it remained in the rough, I knocked my third shot over the green (but not on the road), I chipped up and two-putted for a double-bogey six. I was not upset. I was happy to have finished the hole with the same ball.

To the home hole. Some golfers find Tom Morris, the 354-yard eighteenth, to be an anticlimactic finish, but I am not among them. It is true that the fairway is wider than a football field is long, since the eighteenth fairway is joined with the first. But if you become nervous and fast you can slice your ball out-of-bounds and onto the doorsteps of the clubs and shops along The Links, a road that runs parallel to the hole. It is also true that the hole has no bunkers, but the Valley of Sin, the unforgiving depression in front of the green, is tricky enough. And it is true that the hole has no rough, but putting out with dozens of tourists and townspeople hovering about is rough enough. For world-class players competing in important events, Tom Morris offers a good chance for a birdie three, and that's exciting. I wanted to close with a par, I wanted that bad. I had started the back nine par, par, birdie, par, birdie, and then on fifteen I fell into a three-hole funk: double bogey, bogey, double bogey. I thoroughly believed I could excise that three-hole aberration from my golfing soul if I finished with a par. I brought my trusty Titleist close to my lips, and I said encouraging things to it. With the driver in hand, I aimed for the first tee and swung full and true. I hit the ball well.

For my second shot, I had to decide whether to try to bounce a running shot through the Valley of Sin, or fly a wedge all the way on to the hole. I decided on the latter but hit the pitch tentatively. The ball finished on the green but forty feet short of the hole. Standing on the green, I was nervous: I had attached feelings of self-worth and general importance to my finish, and to my round. My first putt was on line with the hole, but was struck too firmly and it ran five feet past the hole. My eyes were staring down the hole when I knocked that five-footer squarely in. A few onlookers, including Christine, clapped, and my three new friends all said, "Nicely done." I'm sure I was beaming: 45 out, 39 in, 84 on a windy, invigorating day over the Old Course. Christine took another wonderful photograph: George, Paul, William, and me standing on the eighteenth green, putters in hand, smiling cheerfully. In the background, the clubhouse of the Royal and Ancient is bathed in a soft light, and the clock shows half past eight. I asked George to sign my scorecard for verification, and he did so happily, and with care, in his neat Scottish penmanship.

If anything ever happens to the game ball, I still have the scorecard, the pictures, the memories, and, now, this recounting. It is about two A.M. as I write this. I have just returned my mementos to their various places. I'm burning to play.

One more thing about the Old Course. Eighteen has become the standard number of holes for golf courses throughout the world because the Old Course has eighteen holes. But the Old Course has only eleven greens. The first hole has its own green, as do the ninth, the seventeenth, and the eighteenth. Each of the remaining fourteen holes shares a green. There is an excellent mnemonic to remember which holes meet at the green. All the holes that share add up to eighteen. The second and the sixteenth share a green, as do the third and the fifteenth, the fourth and the fourteenth, the fifth and the thirteenth, the sixth and the twelfth, the seventh and the eleventh, and the eighth and the tenth. This becomes particularly interesting if you are familiar with *gematria,* a system of assigning numerical value to words, which has been an elemental part of Judaica since the second century. The number eighteen is symbolically meaningful because it is the numerical equivalent of the Hebrew word *chai,* which means life.

CHAPTER FIFTEEN

GREENKEEPING

IF YOU HEAD EAST OUT OF EDINBURGH on the A198 for twenty miles, along the Firth of Forth—past the Musselburgh Links, past the Royal Musselburgh Golf Club, past the Longniddry Golf Club, past the Kilspindie Golf Club—you will come upon the village of Gullane, a quaint and charming place and home to two thousand souls. In the heart of town, there is a bakery, a newsstand, a couple of banks, a sign to the beach, several pubs, and the clubhouse of the Gullane Golf Club, which has three courses, four if you count a children's course where golf is free. In Gullane, as in most of Scotland, it is not pretentious to begin a sentence with, "At my club. . . ." Half the families in Gullane belong to the Gullane Golf Club, and if they don't they generally belong to Longniddry or Kilspindie or to one of the two clubs in North Berwick, the next big town up the road. If you live in the vicinity of Gullane, and you pay your bills on time, and have never been charged with sheep theft, you can join the Gullane Golf Club. Their membership policy typifies the democratic nature of Scottish golf; the lion's share of Scotland's three hundred and fifty private clubs are run just like the G. G. C.

Which is to say that Gullane's two other clubs are atypical. The Luffness New Golf Club and the Honorable Company of

Edinburgh Golfers practice the kind of elitism typically associated with certain clubs in the south of England, or in Madrid, or almost anywhere in the United States, but not in Scotland. The golf course of the Luffness New Golf Club, routed by Old Tom, is outstanding and obscure, which is how its members want it; the rare visitor there is usually shooed away. Despite its fame, Muirfield, the golf course of the Honorable Company of Edinburgh Golfers and a regular Open venue, is run much the same way. When Americans journey to Scotland to play the historic courses—St. Andrews, followed by Muirfield, Turnberry, Troon, and finishing at Prestwick—they typically don't know Luffness New exists, but they view a game at Muirfield as a trophy. They think that with ingenuity and cunning they can get on. Generally, they are wrong.

Payne Stewart wanted to play Muirfield during a Scottish holiday two weeks after his win in the 1991 U. S. Open at Hazeltine. His request was declined. So instead he played hilly Gullane No. 1, the best of the three good Gullane Golf Club courses. He enjoyed the course's spongy turf, invigorating and gentle underfoot. He enjoyed the sweeping linksland vistas from the peaks of its hills, from which he engaged in a little spying. "I could see that Muirfield was empty," Stewart said later, at the British Open, at Birkdale. "I thought the reason they wouldn't let us play was because they were having a competition or something, but there wasn't a soul on it." He was smiling when he said this, and I had the idea that he was feigning bafflement; Stewart has been around and he's well aware of the ways of the Honorable Company.

I have met men, captains of American industry, who have said they shook in their loafers as they stood before Muirfield's longtime secretary, Captain P. W. T. (Paddy) Hanmer, seeking permission to play. Hanmer, a transplanted Englishman, retired in 1983, but among a certain class of American golfer he remains infamous, and is still today discussed in grill rooms across the United States with fear and awe. If you press them on it, these well-fed capitalists will acknowledge that while they were genuinely intimidated by Hanmer's aloof and brusque English style, they found a certain cryptic pleasure in being treated as groveling dogs. These are men who lead their daily lives with inflated pomp; they grovel for nothing. In that light, appearing before Hanmer was like a return to childhood. "You faced Captain Hanmer as you would face a teacher after class, or your father after you wrecked his car," I was once told. "Carefully."

The secretary at the Luffness New Golf Club, Lt. Col. J. G. Tedford, a Hanmerian scholar, believed that encounters with Hanmer enriched the Muirfield experience for the American visitor. This Hanmer Factor—the feeling of accomplishment and satisfaction in getting past the captain and to the first tee—might be a contributing factor to Muirfield's exalted status. (The course ranked fourth in *Golf* magazine's 1991 list of the one hundred best courses in the world, after Pine Valley, Cypress Point, and Augusta National.) After surviving Hanmer, you made certain that you enjoyed your game.

Hanmer was a career navy man before becoming Muirfield's secretary, a post he held for fifteen years. Tedford was a career army man before he became the Luffness New secretary. As I sat in Tedford's cramped, tidy office one afternoon, I asked him why club secretaries often come from the military. "Because the members want the voice of authority in their lives, and the military man has that voice," Tedford said. "Not just to keep the American visitors in line, but for the sake of the membership and the club. I can say to a senior member, 'Sir, you are no longer able to play off an eighteen handicap—you are now a twenty-one.' From me, he will accept that. If a committeeman told him that, he'd tell him to bugger off. Golf clubs run by committees aren't run at all. That is the lesson of Hanmer. He *ran* Muirfield, ran it with authority."

I wanted to speak with Hanmer, but the very idea made me nervous. Would he tell me the telephone was no way to set up an interview? Would he tell me to bugger off?

"By all means, come over," he said. "Where are you? I'll come pick you up."

"No, that's OK, I can find your house," I said.

"I'll stick a bamboo pole with a red bag on the top in the front yard, so you'll know you have the right house."

I found the house easily, the only one on his suburban block with a bamboo pole, topped by a red seed bag, stuck into the front garden. The house was a stucco bungalow in the heart of Gullane where the captain lived with his sister.

The retired secretary, well into his seventies, greeted me at the door. He was an overweight man with large shaggy ears and he walked with a cane, but he did not lack vibrancy. I had put on a coat and tie for the occasion, and was overdressed. Hanmer was wearing a white golf shirt and khaki pants he apparently used for gardening. In my intimidation, I asked if Hanmer wanted to see a letter of introduction. "Why should I need to see something like that?" he said. I had confused the policies of his former employers with the home life of a long-retired man who had once administered those policies. Hanmer motioned me to a dining room chair. "Sit, sit," he said. "Ask me your questions." Hanmer was direct, and I felt he would appreciate direct questions.

"Most private golf clubs in Scotland act more public than anything else," I said. "Why isn't Muirfield like that?"

"Muirfield is old, and it follows its own tradition," Hanmer said. "In America, private clubs don't allow guest play without a member, and yet Muirfield is criticized for not being more open than it is. We allow visitor play on Tuesdays and Thursdays. If a British golfer went to Florida and tried to play Seminole without a member he wouldn't get past the gate and he would return home with tales of how he was chased away from Seminole by a curmudgeonly security guard in a booth who refused to lift the bar across the foot of the driveway."

Hanmer, it seemed, was describing himself, or how he had been perceived. I asked Hanmer if he knew how he had intimidated some of the supplicants who had appeared before him.

"Let's say I'm aware of the stories that have been told for years," he answered. "I'm aware of how nervous some of them acted. I'm not convinced that any of the shaking was genuine a'tall. They acted the way they thought I expected them to act.

"Look," Hanmer said. He was lecturing, but he was wholly civil. "The days of the upper echelon are over. The class system is all but dead. Look at our prime minister, John Major—he's the son of a circus man. I had butchers and fishermen play the course, and I didn't distinguish between them and the barristers and the businessmen.

"There's no such thing as a gentleman anymore. But when your compatriots came before me, they acted the way they thought a gentleman should act, and I occasionally found it amusing. That's all. So I'd do my bit, too. I'd lift up my binoculars, peer out on the empty course and say, 'I couldn't possibly let you play the course today.' They knew what it meant: it meant that it was a members' day, or that they hadn't made the proper arrangements. There was some fun in it.

"There was once a man from Idaho who came to my office. He asked if he could play the course. I said, 'Sir, how can I let you play the course—you've not made the proper arrangements.' He asked if he could wait. I said, 'How, sir, can I stop you from waiting? I am not an officer of the law.' He asked if there might be a cancellation. I said, 'How do you expect me to know if there will be a cancellation. Do you think I am a swami?' He asked if he could take my picture while he waited. I said, 'Now why in heaven's name would you want my picture?' He said his friends at home would like to see a picture of the man who had stopped him from playing Muirfield. I said, 'That, sir, is the most original approach I have ever heard. Go gather your clubs and play the course.' "

When Hanmer retired from his duties, the club made him an honorary member, and he lunches there weekly. After a long outside search, the club could not find a suitable replacement for Hanmer, so they asked a club member, Major J. G. Vanreenen, to serve as secretary. Vanreenen relinquished his membership and served as secretary for six years; the Honorable Company prohibits members from working for the club. Americans I know who had dealt extensively with both secretaries say they found Vanreenen more aloof and brusque than Hanmer; the undercurrent of playfulness that existed in the Hanmer regime ceased to exist under Vanreenen. In 1990, Vanreenen was reinstated as a member when a suitable successor, Group Captain J. A. Prideaux, was selected. Prideaux is efficient, polite, and fair. A Muirfield tradition has been lost.

"If anybody asks how I'm doing in retirement, just tell them I'm a cripple now," Hanmer said as he showed me to the door. He had said he'd give me an hour, and he gave me exactly that. No tea, no cookies, one hour of direct secretarial talk. "Tell them I've had three hip operations and that I'm on my hands and knees, gardening."

Prideaux was away and I had not made the proper arrangements, so there was no way, short of the miracle of invitation, that I was going to be able to play Muirfield. But I was still hopeful of seeing the course, twelve months before it was to serve as the venue for the one-hundred-and-twenty-first Open. I called up Christopher Whittle, the course superintendent (formerly known as a head greenkeeper), and asked if I might tag along with him as he made his rounds over the course.

There's seldom much interaction between greenkeepers and golfers since the former usually work in the hours just before and after sunrise. Unlike a club professional or a caddie master or a secretary, no greenkeeper gets a job and keeps it by force of personality. A greenkeeper's reputation is built solely on the condition of his course. After he is gone, the fitness of the course during his tenure becomes his legacy.

Whittle was a short, sturdily built man in his mid-thirties—young for such a big job. In the course management business one would be hard-pressed to name a more desirable position than the superintendency at Muirfield, the benefits of which included residence in a beautiful stone house on the Muirfield property and the opportunity to play the course any afternoon, a privilege also extended to the workers on the greenkeeper's crew.

"We have nine men on the crew, and every one of them is a keen golfer, we all play pretty much every night," Whittle told me as we drove around the course in a red jeep. "I tell them to cut the holes wherever they want them—they all know what a good pin position is."

It was a sunny day and the different grasses on the course—chiefly creeping red fescue, chewings fescue, and brown-top bent—blended into an inviting melange of muted greens and browns, not at all like the lush green of American golf in midsummer.

"At some clubs, the greenkeeper has to ask, 'What color do you want the course to be?' And he'll use enough water, seed, and fertilizer to get that color," Whittle said. "That's not how we operate here. We have no sprinklers. Most of the seed is spread naturally, by the wind. We use virtually no fertilizer.

"The members here want the course to be whatever color nature dictates the course should be. If we have a drought, it's brown. If we have a lot of rain, it's green. Usually, it's in between. We have good grass here because we're blessed with good soil. Good soil ages just like good wine. Geologically, this is lucky land."

It was midday and there may have been four or five groups playing. I viewed them enviously.

"Nice, isn't it?" Whittle said. "When I came here for my first interview three years ago I took one look at the golf course and fell in love with it. They invited me back for a second interview. That time I brought my wife. Same exact thing—love at first sight."

We continued our drive, away from the golf course and toward the sea. The Muirfield course never meets the beach, which is why some people think it lacks charm. Whittle showed me what exists between the course and Gullane Bay.

There is a wide, long stretch of sand dunes, one after another, covered with long thick blades of beach grass. The sunlight glimmered off these blades and when the sea breeze swept through they rippled like sequins on a party dress. You could see ships at sea. You could hear the sea gulls. If John Stark were here, I thought, he'd be happy. This was linksland. This land was *alive.*

Our eyes pored over the virgin dunes. The architect in me was at work. "This may be the finest stretch of golfing land God ever created," Whittle said. "This is the great dilemma of this club. Do you build a golf course and make what could be one of the best courses in the world? Or is that too much—is it too much for one club to have two of the best courses in the world? We already have a very special place in golf. Do you risk diluting all that's special here by building more?"

We drove back toward the clubhouse, discussing that tract of land. I was wondering about the possibility of a wholly natural course on it, a course tended largely by sheep. I didn't get a chance to ask Whittle about that, for we had arrived back near the clubhouse and there was a man there waiting for him.

"Did you get a fourth for our game tonight?" the man wanted to know.

"No," Whittle said, "did you?"

"No, I thought you were going to."

There was some discussion over who would complete their fourball that night when Whittle turned to me and asked, "Did you want to play with us tonight?"

I tried to stay calm: had I just been invited for a round at Muirfield? I felt tingly. "Absolutely," I said.

"Great," he said.

Yes!

"Do you know where the East Links in North Berwick is?"

North Berwick? East Links? My heart sank. No words were forthcoming.

"That's where we're going to play tonight. Can you find it?"

I nodded yes.

"Good. We'll see you there at six."

An invitation to Muirfield still eluded me.

At six, we met up again. To determine partners, we threw balls. It was Law Hardy, a roofing contractor with enormous hands, and me against greenkeeper Whittle and Dave Middleton, a policeman in the town of Dunbar. Law and I won the front nine, halved the back, and won the match. I was a guest of the three members. There were no stakes; the only thing that mattered was the outcome of the game.

Chris, a lefty, was a serious-minded player. Dave, the bobby, was just the opposite. When one man was up, the other was down and they managed a team par on just about every hole. But Law and I had a couple of birdies each and that was the difference. We won.

The four of us holed our final putts in the calm of the day's final light. A mass of cool air came out of the dusk while a sweet-scented warmth emanated from the earth. I felt so completely alert. When I took my ball out of the eighteenth hole, I noticed that my feet were warm, my nose was cold, and my golf ball was wet with dew. It was a fine night of golf, played over a good linksland course. I don't think a game at Muirfield could have been any better. Certainly, at Muirfield, we would not have been able to retire to the clubhouse after our round, as we did that night on the East Links in North Berwick.

The dress code in the East Links clubhouse required only that entrants not wear spikes. The barman, a member himself, knew what Chris wanted without his having to ask. The green-keeper, the *golfer,* stood in his socks and had a pint of his favorite lager, enjoying the pleasures of a finished game and the privileges of membership. Muirfield was just down the road and a world away.

We stayed nearly two weeks in East Lothian, the seaside county in which Gullane is located, and I played up and down the coast-line. When Christine made a side trip through Northern Ireland with her visiting sister, Claire, I played twice a day. My favorite courses were Gullane No. 1; the west course in North Berwick; and, another six miles down the road, Dunbar East, not to be confused with Dunbar Winterfield. After each game, I wrote in a notebook, describing the course, the condition of my game, and the people with whom I played. When my playing partners had particularly admirable swings, I'd ask them to tell me their best swing thought, what they considered to be the most important tenet of the swing, and I'd record that in the note-book, too.

"Follow through to one o'clock," I wrote after a game with George Waites, a silver-haired retired rugby coach with whom I had played several games over Gullane No. 1 and No. 2. George wanted to make sure that after contact with the ball his clubhead continued on a path away from his body. Such a swing path, he said, promotes a draw and prohibits your body from becoming lazy during the swing, both desirable goals. I found his thought helpful.

"Don't start your downswing until you can see your backswing," I wrote after a round with Melinda Shawn, a New Zealander on holiday with whom I played the west course in North Berwick. Melinda was referring to a critical moment in the swing, between the backswing and the downswing, when there should be an instantaneous pause. In that moment of limbo, the backswing concludes and the downswing commences. To ensure that she paused, Melinda did not start her downswing until she could see her clubhead from the corner of her left eye at the top of her backswing. I found that helpful, too.

"Imagine yourself holing your shot before you play it," I wrote after going around Dunbar with a teenager named Duncan Drysdale. Duncan cited an example from his recent past. He was playing at Royal Musselburgh, trying to qualify for a winter golf league, and he needed to shoot 84 or better. His day was not going well and after the thirteenth hole he needed to play the remaining five holes in two over par to shoot his 84. He made a double bogey on fourteen and a bogey on fifteen. Now he needed to play the remaining three holes in one under par to shoot 84. He made a par on sixteen. He made a par on seventeen. He pushed his second on the par-four eighteenth into a greenside pot bunker. "As I went into the bunker, I could see in my mind the shot rattling against the pin and falling in," he said. And that, of course, is what happened. Duncan's swing thought—to imagine holing your shot before you play it—has been rattling against my brain ever since.

I enjoyed thoroughly the golf in the East Lothian district, which means I enjoyed thoroughly the combination of golf courses and golfers I encountered. But nothing left more of an impression on me than those untouched sandhills between the edge of the Muirfield course and Gullane Bay. I knew of nothing in golf that would be more beautiful than a series of eighteen holes routed through those dunes. My course there would be an essentially unknown links, with greens cut by hand mowers and fairways maintained by sheep, with holes laid out by the dictates of the dunes. The obstacles would be indigenous: beach grass, sand, and wind. I wondered if such a course existed anywhere. If it did, I wondered if I would ever find it.

Christine and I sat in our packed car, trying to decide where to go next. We were traveling by whim, not itinerary. We had maps, brochures, guidebooks, notes, and clippings strewn about the front seat. Should we head for Boat of Garten? Should we visit the Isle of Skye? Should we go to the islands of Rhum and Eigg? I found a telephone and called Stark, seeking counsel. I told him about my experiences in East Lothian. I told him about the sandhills off Muirfield. I told him about my dream for a course there. And he said, "You're ready for Cruden Bay."

I had heard of Cruden Bay once before. A friend from Philadelphia, Jim Finegan, widely traveled in golf, a discerning but wildly enthusiastic man, had written about the course for *Golf Journal,* a publication of the United States Golf Association. He described Cruden Bay as "golfing country of rare splendor; in truth, of undeniable majesty, for in my experience these sandhills are the mightiest in Scotland, rising some forty, even sixty feet, their slopes covered with the long and strangling bents that spell disaster to the off-target stroke. This is heroic ground. . . ." After reading Finegan's piece for the first time some years back, I looked for mentions of Cruden Bay in books. I could find not a sentence about it in *The Golf Course,* a vast and comprehensive tome, nor in *The World Atlas of Golf,* also a book of encyclopedic dimension, nor in *The World of Golf,* another heavyweight. It didn't make *The Good Golf Guide,* a compendium of what Peter Alliss regards as the two hundred best courses in the British Isles. There was nothing about it in *The Golf Courses of the British Isles,* by Bernard Darwin, nor in *A Round of Golf Courses,* foreword by

Bernard Darwin. (If you don't know who Darwin is, find something, anything, by him.) I wondered then: might Cruden Bay be another Finegan enthusiasm?

But here was Stark sending me to Cruden Bay. I dug out a copy of Finegan's piece from the clipping file I had been carrying throughout the trip. I sat in the front seat of our car and reread the story with new appreciation, for not only did it describe the place Stark recommended, but it also painted the very thing I had seen in the dunes off Muirfield's fifth—rare splendor, undeniable majesty, heroic ground! We were off.

We drove through Edinburgh, over the Forth Road Bridge, north on the M90 to Perth, up the A92 through Aberdeen, two-thirds of the way up the east coast of Scotland. Finally, four hours after we had left, we turned onto the two-lane beach road that led us into the village of Cruden Bay. That night, and twice a day for the next few days, I played Cruden Bay. Finegan and Stark were right: the course was awesome.

It was unlike any course I had ever seen before. While the terrain of the Old Course rolled like the swells of a bay, the Cruden Bay landscape resembled a stormy ocean. Often, you played off cliffs and into greens either surrounded by dunes or perched on the tops of hills. The wind—heavy, chilly, and wet—was a constant consideration.

The course called for all types of shot-making, including some quirky shots that I had never before seen, not even at St. Andrews. The approach shot to the par-four second hole required a pitch to a firm plateau green, which sloped away from the fairway. With the hole cut in the front of the green, the only way to get your ball near it was to bounce your shot up the face of the hill, a weird and interesting play. The third was a downhill par-four of 286 yards on which par was an exceptionally pleasing score. My regular Cruden Bay partners, local lads named Marshall Birnie and Gary Duncan, showed me how to play the approach shot there, bouncing it off three key mounds, pinball-style.

From the tenth tee, a burn 260 yards away was within the reach of most players, since you played from a tee box eighty feet above the fairway, and your drive hurtled through the air.

The thirteenth green was protected by a huge dune right in front of it, sitting there like a big sleeping guard dog, over which you lobbed your third shot (provided you had played your first two according to plan). The fifteenth was a blind dogleg par-three, 239 yards from the back tee. It was a poorly designed hole, but a fun one. There was not a hole without character, and not a moment on the course when you weren't in the thick of great linksland.

The names of the holes, even though they were mostly in the old Aberdeenshire dialect that is nearly extinct today, were still meaningful. Going out you played Slains, Crochdane, Claypits, Port Erroll, The Buck, Bluidy Burn, Whaupshank, Ardendraught, and Hawklaw. Coming in you played Scaurs, Mishanter, Finnyfal, Bents, Whins, Blin' Dunt, Coffins, Bilin' Wallie, and Hame. Slains is the name of a castle in Cruden Bay, a castle Bram Stoker used as a setting for *Dracula.* The burn that runs through the course got its name, Bluidy, from a battle on the linksland between Danes and Scots in the year 1012; the blood of the dead and near-dead drained into the burn and its water ran red for days. Crochdane means slayer of the Danes.

The origins of the course were more festive. Like many nineteenth-century Scottish courses, the Cruden Bay Golf Club owed its founding to the ambitiousness of a recreation-bent railway company. Long before golf went there, Cruden Bay already had strong appeal. It had two miles of crescent-shaped sandy beach; dramatic cliffs; and towering sand dunes; a lively, picturesque fishing fleet; and the Slains Castle. The daring minds at the Great North of Scotland Railway Company figured that if they could build a train line to Cruden Bay, and a palatial hotel with a first-rate golf course, they would make money on train tickets, room charges, and green fees. For a while, the plan worked splendidly and Cruden Bay was a smart holiday resort. But the First World War put a dent in business and neither the train line nor the hotel lasted through the Second. Only the golf course survived. It was a gem.

Yet my search for perfect linksland could not stop in Cruden Bay. It was not the golfing place of my dreams, for two reasons:

it wasn't undiscovered, and it didn't have a true and great golf ambiance. The British came from all corners of their kingdom to play Cruden Bay. Also, the oil drilling in the North Sea—with rigs visible from the hills of the golf course—attracted Americans by the score. They came for the oil, and soon after discovered the golf. I never had the idea that golf was central to life in Cruden Bay, as I had in Gullane and St. Andrews and in John Stark's office. Golf was brought to Cruden Bay to add to its allure as a resort, and nearly one hundred years later I think that fact still influenced the feel of the place. In time, I'm sure, that will change: Christine and I attended a Saturday night barbecue at the club, and among the younger members there was some *serious* golf talk, including a shrewd analysis of some of the weaker holes on the back nine. A few years back, the members did a smart thing: they changed the name of their club from the Cruden Bay Golf and Country Club to the Cruden Bay Golf Club. Someday, I think, it will evolve into a place with real golf spirit.

My last round there was like my last game on the Old Course—all-consuming. I had a chance of breaking 80, something that I had still not done since that fleeting summer between high school and college. I went out in 40 and needed a four on the par-four Hame hole to shoot 39 coming in, for 79, nine over par. On the eighteenth, I hit a weak, bouncy drive and a weak second to the front edge of the green. The pin was in the back. My first putt finished six feet short of the hole. My putt for 79 went two feet past the hole and never touched it. Even my third putt didn't drop. Four putts for 81. An inglorious finish—Cruden Bay deserved far better.

We packed up and hit the road. There was still much to learn and much to see.

CHAPTER SIXTEEN

Auchnafree

STARK'S OFFICE IN CRIEFF was on the way between Cruden Bay, in the northeast of Scotland, and Glasgow, our next destination, in the southwest. After my loathsome use of the short stick in Cruden Bay, I asked Stark if I might come in for a putting lesson. He hesitated, and then said yes.

"Putting is a game within the game," Stark said as we stood on the practice putting green of the Crieff Golf Club. Under his arm was an old hickory-shafted blade putter, and two Ping putters of recent vintage. "I believe there are people preternaturally disposed to putting well, but I am not one of them," he said, explaining his hesitation at my request for a putting lesson.

"When I came back from Sweden and took the professional's job here, nearly thirty years ago now, I wanted to play well in the Scottish tournaments, our so-called Tartan Tour. To the Scottish club professional, winning Scottish tournaments is like a university professor being published in the scholarly journals: it's good for the pro, it's good for his club. I knew I had to improve my putting. So I'd stand on this green until I had made two hundred consecutive three-footers. *Two hundred.* By the time I'd get to one ninety-nine, I'd be sick, literally sick, I'd feel so much pressure. I stood on this green for hours, well into darkness.

In time I developed a fascination for putting, but I didn't have an innate fascination for it. I don't know that the *art* of putting is learnable, but I think anybody can train themselves to be a better putter."

I loved being in John Stark's presence, hearing him rolling his Rs, "*arrrt*," as he talked about the game. He was an engaging man, a knowledgeable man. Although his formal education had concluded when he was fifteen, I sensed he had an abiding interest in academia, and he definitely had a fondness for the word *scholarly*. He once told me that Nicklaus was "the best player of all time, and the most scholarly—that tells you something." But to me, Stark was the scholarly one. Not in appearance; he always looked like a guy off to see his bookmaker. But in word and in deed. J. M. Stark was Professor of Golf, with subspecialties in the game's history, psychology, and philosophy.

Stark looked at my putter, a heavy, clumsy-looking Spalding with a stubby toe and a pointed heel. Its price tag was still taped to the shaft. "Sixty bucks," Stark said, and he whistled. "A charitable donation." The Spalding was new to my bag. I wished I had brought my old putter with me, a hickory-shafted, leather-gripped, mallet-headed Otey Crisman, made in Selma, Alabama, circa 1960. I had used that putter from my first year in the game, 1974, through 1990, when in a fit of mean-spiritedness and impulsiveness I retired it. Throughout my thirteen-year slump, putting was never the root of my problem. But when my game bottomed out in the summer of 1990, I started lashing out in all directions. Out went my leather-gripped steel-shafted MacGregor Super Eye-O-Matic Tourney driver, with its beautiful bleached persimmon head (now a paperweight). In went a jet-black graphite-shafted, graphite-headed, rubber-gripped Yonex, the Carbonex II model, a Darth Vader of a driver. Also summarily dismissed, despite years of faithful service, were my 1971 Wilson Staff irons, the bullet-back model, with their steel shafts and leather grips, bought used in 1977 for one hundred dollars, replaced by a set of graphite-shafted, rubber-gripped Japanese-made PRGRs, the CT-440 model, costing ten times more than their predecessors. Finally, to complete the purge, the beautiful Otey Crisman, much beloved and rich in memories, was buried unceremoniously in a closet, and replaced with the ugly but much-touted Spalding. As I stood on that green in Crieff, hearing my mentor call my new putter a "damned battle-ax," I missed the old Otey a great deal, and I could not understand why we had ever had a falling out.

Stark asked me to describe my putting problems. I told him that I hadn't fully appreciated how bad my putting was until Cruden Bay, where I started counting putts. In my last round there, the 81, forty of my strokes were putts, including the four-putt on the last green. Any golfer beyond the level of novice should not take more than thirty-six putts per round, two per green on average. Touring professionals seldom take more than thirty-two.

"Your ball-striking had improved then," Stark said.

"Oh, definitely," I blurted out. I was embarrassed for a moment by my immodesty. But then I realized I was also complimenting my teacher. "In my last round at Cruden Bay, I hit thirteen greens in regulation." That means I reached thirteen of the greens in the hole's par, less two strokes. Hitting a par-five in regulation means you took three strokes to reach the green. If you hit a green in regulation, you should make no worse than par.

"And to what do you attribute your improved ball-striking?" Stark asked.

"Many things. Being in Scotland. Being immersed in the game. Playing so many good courses. Lack of distraction. Learning to hear the swing, learning to breathe during the swing. Being determined to improve."

"That's good," Stark said. "That's all good. Now apply all those things to your putting, and your putting will come around, too. Don't forget that putting is also ball-striking. Stick with that idea of hearing the lovely sounds of good golf. It's more easily accomplished in putting than in any other part of the game.

"On you go, now, take some putts, and listen carefully for the sound your ball makes when it strikes the face of the putter."

Stark handed me the old hickory-shafted putter. I thought

about the sound of contact, to the exclusion of everything else. I had never before done that with putting. It was amazing. When I struck a putt even slightly off line, a dull sound resulted. Putts struck well made a discernibly more pleasant sound. How could I have never before noticed such a phenomenon? I found that I didn't have to concentrate on the mechanics of the stroke, all I had to focus on was re-creating the sound of good contact. When I did that, the rest, the technical requirements of a proper putting stroke, occurred naturally.

And that, I have come to realize, was the essence of Stark's teaching theory, at least the one he employed for me: if a stroke—be it a drive, iron shot, pitch, chip, bunker shot, or putt—produced a good sound, then all the mechanics must have been good. Good mechanics produced good shots. Stark's teaching encouraged a pupil's instincts to take over.

The golf swing is not as unnatural as adults make it out to be. If you place a golf club in the hands of a ten-year-old, show her a sound grip, and instruct her to keep her feet steady, she will as often as not make a solid swing. She may not make good contact, because the eye-hand coordination of a ten-year-old is not usually well developed, but the shape of her swing will be classical, in the tradition of Bobby Jones or Glenna Collett Vare. Once you have a good grip and a good stance, the swing *is* instinctive. This is especially applicable to putting: most touring professionals I have talked to, including Johnny Miller, Seve Ballesteros, and Billy Casper, were *sure* they had done their best putting as kids, when they didn't think about putting technique at all.

Stark was a cerebral man, a man who read the great poets for recreation. But he was not teaching me cerebral golf. He was teaching me native golf. He believed that if a player concentrated on a single thing—producing pleasing sounds, in my case—everything else would follow. That was his way of eliminating the complexity adults introduce to the game. I strove to follow his teachings. That afternoon, I stayed on the practice putting green for hours, trying to improve my percussions.

Late in the day, Stark came out of his shop. "Still at it, that's good, Michael," he said. "You may find the fascination for putting yet. The game within the game, it is. There have been many with consuming interest for golf who never developed an intrigue for putting. Hogan was such a man. Of course, putting is more of the game now than it was ever before. In the Scottish golf of my youth, we didn't worry so about putting. The greens were rougher then, and there was only so much good putting you could do on them. We figured the blown sand and tufts of grass were as likely to knock your ball on line as off." Stark stopped, placed his right index finger on his chin and lower lip and looked down at his shoes, and then up.

"I have a thought, Michael, I have a thought. Why don't you come by tomorrow morning. There's something I'd like to show you, something I think you'll enjoy seeing. Bring your clubs. I'm going to take you to someplace very special, a place where no American has gone before, I am quite sure of that."

The next morning, I put my clubs in the back of Stark's silver Volvo station wagon, and we drove out of the parking lot and onto the winding narrow roads and into the lush green Scottish summer. Stark didn't tell me where we were headed, and I didn't ask. His demeanor was solemn, although his clothes were not: he wore his white loafers, a white golf shirt, and fire-engine red pants, held up, in a manner of speaking, by a white belt. I had never before seen red pants that bright, and I thought about Teravainen's belief that red was a dangerous and powerful color. Embroidered on the right front pocket of Stark's trousers was the shield of the town of St. Andrews, depicting a robed Saint Andrew, the patron saint of Scotland, carrying the X-shaped cross on which he was crucified. We drove for a few miles on the main road to Perth, and then turned onto a smaller, rougher road. The countryside was undeveloped and magnificent.

There was no conversation for a while. Then Stark said, "What did you think of Cruden Bay?"

I was glad to hear him talk. "I thought the golf course was wonderful," I replied, "but I didn't find magic there."

"Aye." He paused. "Where we're going, there's magic."

I tried to keep up a calm appearance. "Are we going to a golf course?" I asked slowly.

"Yes," Stark said.

I paused, in the manner of Stark. "Have I heard of it?"

"No."

I wondered if he would take one more question.

"What's it called?" I asked.

A Stark pause. "Auchnafree," he said. He pronounced the *ch* in the Scots manner, as a soft guttural sound, pushing air from his lungs to the top of his throat, and trapping it there for a split-second by momentarily lodging the tip of his tongue below his lower teeth. I had been traveling for so long that I had lost the sensation of being abroad, but at that moment I felt keenly aware of being in a foreign land.

We pulled off the secondary road and onto a dirt road, and we drove on for many miles. The land was inhabited only by sheep and rabbits, and the air was inhabited by birds. A river ran parallel to the road. Except for the road, there was no evidence of human life. "This road is an ancient way," Stark said. He pointed with his thick fingers. "That is the River Almond. Years ago, you would have found the wee little houses of the shepherds here. They lived up and down this glen. Before the days of electricity here, if you lived on the banks of the Almond, you were rich. Nobody wants that life today. That life is considered too hard now. Scotland's become civilized." His tone suggested he did not view this development favorably.

Stark pulled off the road and got out. The land was vast and treeless, like a plain. It was covered with vegetation, like an English heathland, but there wasn't enough peat or shrubbery on it to be true heathland. For the most part, the land was covered with grass. It was the rich grass of suburban dreams, not the kind of grass you would have expected to see in so rugged a setting. If you had grass like that in your backyard, or on the fairways of your home course, you'd be thrilled. With little movements of his big head, Stark looked approvingly at the hills, the sky, the river, the grass. He smiled.

The land, Stark explained, was owned by a man named Sir

James Whitaker, who maintained an estate deep in the hills. For many years the estate had had a shepherd named John Pollock, who had been a close friend of Stark's. He pointed to a boulder, onto which a plaque had been bolted. It read:

JOHN POLLOCK
SHEPHERD
1940——1990

"John Pollock was a member at Crieff, but this is where he lived and this was his true home course, in this glen called Auchnafree," Stark said. "John was a good player, and he loved the game. Dead only a year now. He had tried to save one of his sheep from drowning in the river, and he drowned himself. He was a strong man, but he didn't know how to swim. I remember at the funeral, his mother did not cry. I won't forget that. She was weeping inside, I'm sure, but she did not cry, the old Scot." For a moment, Stark silently remembered that day, and his friend.

"John Pollock laid out a six-hole course in this glen. He picked a superb spot. This is the finest turf on which I have ever struck a golf ball. We played two tournaments here each year: the Auchnafree Open and the Auchnafree-St. Davids match. I'd captain St. Davids; that's my village. John captained Auchnafree. You'd play the course three times, and between each six you'd go to the river and get out your flask and a glass and fix yourself up with a wee drink."

The river babbled and sparrows sang. I thought of the sparrows as gulls and the river as a sea, and in that light the geological identity of the land was plain: it was linksland, no question about it. I'm certain Stark saw it that way, too.

After my first visit with Stark, I had thought he might be regretful that his home course, Crieff, was a parkland course, and not a linksland course. Now I knew that if my thought was right, then Auchnafree was his antidote. Auchnafree—undiscovered, primal, pure—was his linksland, it was his golfing haven. As he looked about the glen, his pleasure was irrepressible. I had never before seen his moods change the way they did on this day.

"I'd like you to play the course," Stark said to me. "It'll be good for you, good for your education." I was elated. "I'm curious to see what kind of shape the course is in. It'll be a little rough now, I'm sure; it hasn't been played since John's death.

"We plan to play the Auchnafree Open in the fall. We'll have to cut the greens, but this course needs little from the hand of man. Just some tin cans for holes, and flagsticks. It rains daily in this glen, so the grass is always green. The sheep cut and fertilize the fairways, and they build the bunkers. Natural bunkers, you know? All the sheep want to do is protect themselves from the wind and the cold, and in the process they make our game bloody more difficult, and bloody more interesting."

The bunkers on Scottish golf courses do not look like the bunkers on American courses, where they are typically shallow depressions filled with fluffy sand. In Scotland, the bunkers have walls and the sand is often coarse. When Christopher Whittle took me around Muirfield he told me that one of his most important winter tasks was the "revetting" of the bunker walls with bricks of sod. They worked hard at Muirfield to make the bunkers look natural, and after visiting Auchnafree I understood how successful they were.

I walked past the John Pollock memorial boulder and to the first tee. The tee markers were small rocks, painted white. The flagsticks were not even a yard high and their flags were tattered from years of flapping in the breeze. In their uncut state, the greens were barely distinguishable from the fairways—you had to chip your way to the hole, so I didn't have the opportunity to apply my new putting thoughts. But it was unforgettable golf. You teed up among the dandelions and the boulders and the harmless piles of sheep dung. The ball flew fantastically well in the air of that glen and sat invitingly on its lively turf. Each hole had a natural design to it. The opener was a medium-length par-three, followed by a par-four of about three hundred and ninety yards, with the River Almond running down the lefthand side. The third was a short uphill par-three and the fourth a long sidehill par-three. The fifth was a short par-four where my errant shot sent the sheep scattering (as almost any shot could, for sheep abounded). The best hole was the last, the sixth, a par-four of about three hundred and thirty yards. From an elevated tee you played for a narrow valley below and there was little room for error: if you sliced the ball wildly, you'd be on the road or possibly in the river; if you hooked the ball you'd be on a hill too steep for the sheep, where the grass was hearty and unplayable.

Stark had not planned to play; his arthritic hip had been acting up, and he was uncomfortable. But once I began, he joined right in. I felt I should tee up his ball for him, as Old Tom Morris had done for the captains of the Royal and Ancient. Stark would have none of that. He grunted and put his peg in the ground, and grunted on his backswing. He was in pain.

My modern clubs seemed ill-suited to the setting, but Stark swung them without comment or complaint, and swung them well. His shots made the same pleasing sounds they did when we had our first practice session together. His ball flight had a gentle little draw, what he called his "Scottish hook." When Stark hit a poor shot off the third tee he said, "Another ball please." He got off the next one beautifully, launching one of Teravainen's old Titleist 384s, stamped with an 8, into the sweet Auchnafree air.

We didn't talk much. There was no discussion of technique (I was making good shots) or professional golf (that had not been invented yet) or anything about the world away from Auchnafree. We kept no score.

But I know what I made on the last, and I know that Stark knows, too. I walloped a drive, pitched to fifteen feet, and holed my chip with a 6-iron—the most satisfying birdie of my life. When my ball went in, Stark called out, "Master!"

I felt intoxicated. Not only because I had made a birdie, and not only because I had had the chance to show my teacher that all his good efforts were not in vain, but because I had come so far, in every regard. At the age of thirty-one, I had rekindled all the feelings of excitement for the game I had known as a schoolboy. All the clutter that impedes the game in the United States—the golf carts, the expensiveness, the slowness, the social trappings—vanished from mind and memory. Through Stark, I had discovered real golf, and I was a happy man. Shepherd Pollock was the original golfer, and his flock's grazing land, Auchnafree, the original links. Pollock was the pathfinder, the original settler. I had followed in his footsteps. Stark had taken me to a place where I could shed my former selves and start anew. Auchnafree was an Eden, a six-hole Eden.

CHAPTER SEVENTEEN

Machrihanish

AFTER THAT SIX-HOLE GAME on the green pastures of Auchnafree, I could have contentedly gone home, but Stark suggested otherwise. He said I should think of the shepherd's course as part of a trilogy: Auchnafree, Machrihanish, Dornoch. Dornoch was faintly famous, and highly regarded. But Machrihanish was an unknown. I knew that Finegan had been, and Stark, but other than those two robust souls, nobody I knew had set cleated foot there. It never came up in conversation; it never came up in reading; it never came up.

Christine was happy—she was in favor of anything that extended the length of our trip. When we were in Malta she said, "Let's live here." When we were in France she said, "Let's live here." Now it was Scotland's turn. We got out the maps. To find Dornoch you just kept sliding your finger up the well-defined northeastern coast until you crossed the Dornoch Firth. Machrihanish was a different matter. We knew it was a seaside village on a southwestern peninsula called Kintyre, but the coastline in that part of Scotland is discombobulated and Kintyre was slow to emerge. In looking for Kintyre we found a lot of competition for our attention: the island of Arran (to the east, it turned out), the islands Gigha, Islay, and Jura (to the west), and Ireland (to the south) are all in the neighborhood. The Kintyre peninsula was found dangling off the palm of Scotland like a dislocated finger. Machrihanish, on our map, was a speck, too small to accommodate its long and lyrical name (which is pronounced with the same soft guttural *ch* as Auchnafree and Dornoch). Machrihanish was on the west coast of Kintyre near the peninsula's southernmost tip. It looked out of the way, and that fact, of course, only encouraged us. We were on our way.

The journey down Kintyre—on the A83, which runs directly along the Atlantic coastline—was breathtaking, except at its concluding point, in the middle-sized burgh of Campbeltown, a once-thriving coal, fish, and whisky town that lost its economic base when the world marketplace lost its patience for small-scale production. From Campbeltown it was another six miles along a country road to our destination, farmland all the way. Machrihanish was the end of the line—a village comprised of a few dozen houses, all hugging the shore; a general store; a defunct resort hotel converted into flats; a bar; the modest white-stucco clubhouse of the Machrihanish Golf Club; and the course. A quiet place, yet our nine days there were crowded, and whizzed by in a blur. Machrihanish became for me a golfing Nirvana. If I were allowed to play only one course for the rest of my life, Machrihanish would be the place.

Where do I begin to try to explain the joys of Machrihanish? It was remote and undiscovered and that implies a great deal immediately (uncrowded, inexpensive), but what else? Do I start by introducing the art dealer from San Francisco, a scratch player, who was lured by the euphonious name and stayed? Or should you first meet Mr. Peter Kelly, a native son and a friend of Stark's who, after having studied the Machrihanish links for six decades, concluded that the course would never be entirely knowable, a fact that delighted and encouraged him? Or would you first like to hear about the Old Folks' Open and the eloquence of its surprise winner? Maybe I ought to outline the course's distinguished lineage. Or should I describe the sunsets over the ocean, in which the world turned to orange and blue? Or our bed-and-breakfast, across the road from the eighteenth hole, run by the captain of the club and his wife, with a front lawn maintained like a putting green? Or the superb fresh fish dishes served in the clubhouse, accompanied by vegetables straight out of Peter Kelly's garden? Or with the course itself?

I'll start with the course, but only in general terms, because I don't want to spoil the thrill of discovery for you if you ever make it there. It was a course that brought out the best in my game, a course sublime in its natural beauty, a course that moved Old Tom Morris to say (according to Peter Kelly), "The Almichty maun hae had gowf in his e'e when he made the place." Like the artist who discovers the sculpture buried within a slab of granite, the early Machrihanish golfers unearthed the ambrosial course hidden within the great Machrihanish linksland. I was there in the memorable summer, when the links were sweet with the scent of wild orchids and thyme, commingling with the brackish breath of the ocean and the sweat of a golfer trying to conquer himself.

The tee for the first hole, a long par-four called Battery, was outside the pro shop (which was slightly larger and more permanent than a shack) on a bluff above the beach of Machrihanish Bay (in calm times) or the Atlantic Ocean (after major storms). The opening drive required you to play a drive over beach or ocean, depending on the level of sea, and the state of your game.

The second shot on the second, another long par-four, called for an uphill shot to a blind green. Modernists and others who think golf should be "fair," and who are therefore opposed to "blind" shots—a shot in which you cannot see all of a hole's obstacles—will dislike Machrihanish, which has half a dozen such shots. I love blind shots; I think there is little in golf more fun than making what feels like a good strike and then eagerly charging up to the crest of a hill to see if your feeling is justified. Tommy Armour, the U. S. and British Open champion, once told Pete Dye, the golf-course designer, that a blind shot is blind only once to a golfer with memory. I think that's a valuable thought.

From the third to the eighth, Machrihanish was pure duneland. Every tee, every fairway, and every green was either on the plateau of a dune or in a valley between dunes. Nothing was linear, a constant reminder that the golf course was part of the earth, not an artificial creation unto itself. From the tee of the third hole, a longish par-four, you drove toward a peak on the island of Islay. On the fourth, a short par-three, the tee was on the top of one dune and the green atop another, 120 yards away. On the fifth, called Punch Bowl, a 385-yard two-shotter, you coaxed your tee shot to a little saucer at the bottom of the fairway. On the sixth, a par-four of only 315 yards, you prayed for your tee shot to carry a towering dune on the fairway's starboard side. The seventh was a bear, 432 yards long, with a blind second shot over another monstrous dune, where the local custom was for a playing partner to stand on the top of the dune, to monitor your approach shot. If you fetched the green, a thumb shot in the air. If you did not, your scout signaled nothing at all, leaving you to run up the hill and discover your own fate. Before leaving the seventh green for the eighth tee, you rang a bell, to let the players behind you know that the way was clear. The bell-ringing was largely superfluous, since the course was ordinarily empty, but you did it anyway: it was part of the ritual. From the eighth tee, another two-shotter, you saw everything: the islands, the ocean, the beach, the grass-covered dunes, the neighboring airfield of the Royal Air Force, and the twisting fairways and curvaceous greens.

The ninth, a shortish par-four, was the only hole where you could be distracted by R.A.F. activity; it abutted a runway.

The next two holes, the par-five tenth and the par-three eleventh, were of unclassifiable length, because they had numerous teeing grounds, so the lengths of the hole were constantly varied, a sound and simple design concept seldom employed by modern golf-course architects.

The twelfth was an outstanding three-shotter. On a map of the course, the Long Hole appeared to be a straightaway par-five. But after several tries you realized the hole had to be treated as a double dogleg. The good tee shot was played to the far right of the fairway to set up a second shot to the left. From there, you had the chance to bounce your third through the lone opening to the green.

The second shot to the thirteenth hole, a par-four of 370

yards, required inventiveness. The green was hard and sloped away from the fairway. The proper shot required you to land your ball, with just the right steam, in front of the hill that protected the green.

The fourteenth was the longest par-four on the course, measuring 442 yards, with only one tiny bunker on the entire hole. There were long-defunct coal-mining tunnels protruding from under the fairway, creating the appearance of a submarine burial ground and resulting in strange stances.

The fifteenth and sixteenth were an unusual pair: back-to-back par-threes. The sixteenth measured 233 yards, and it was the easier of the two. The fifteenth, seemingly relatively tame at 167 yards, had a plateau green that sloped from right to left. If you missed the green left, you faced a testing pitch from a grassy lie and up a steep embankment. The sixteenth offered little relief; it called for a wooden club for practically everybody. However, if your tee shot didn't finish on the green, it was not a difficult bogey. You could not say that of the fifteenth.

The only letdown came on the final two holes, both shortish par-fours with out-of-bounds demarcations down the left side of their fairways, which bordered the pleasant nine-holer that adjoined the main course. Aside from the artificial out-of-bounds, the seventeenth was a fine hole, but the eighteenth, I'm afraid, was just an ordinary golf hole, the only ordinary hole on the course.

Like Muirfield, Machrihanish has a substantial sweep of unused duneland, and I think the day will come when they will discover a new hole—a par-four, I suspect—in the large stretches of land that exist between the beach and parts of the front nine. In conjunction with that discovery, I think, the club will find a way to combine the existing final two holes and create a spectacular par-five home hole. That would change the course from a par 70 to a par 71 and lengthen the course from 6,228 yards to maybe 6,500 yards.

But if they never do a thing, that won't be news, for golfers are always resistant to change on their own course. We tend to feel an emotional stake in any hole we come to know well. The hole becomes bound in memory, part of our lives. If you know how to play a hole particularly well, the devotion can become paranormal, even allowing for the mammal tendency toward attachment. Anyway, the members of Machrihanish—which is to say anybody in the area who likes golf (mostly everybody) and who can afford the annual dues of one hundred and forty pounds (ditto)—already have an exquisite course.

It was a natural course, kept up by a four-man greenkeeping crew working with a tiny budget. They used no herbicides, and as a result, wildflowers proliferated. There was nothing mechanized about Machrihanish. The greens—lively, fast, oddly shaped, whimsically sloped, and covered with dense, hearty grass—were cut when the greenkeeper decided they needed cutting. The same was true for the fairways, which were nearly as spongy underfoot as the turf at Auchnafree. There was no schedule for anything, a function of the casual nature of the place. There were video games and a big color television in the clubhouse, and binoculars at the bar, used to spy on matches in progress. The social life of the village revolved around the club; the clubhouse was like a den.

Machrihanish was not a grueling course, but any legitimate scratch golfer who went around on a breezy day in level fours (the Scottish phrase for averaging four shots per hole) would be extremely delighted. And yet I don't think a twenty-handicapper would ever struggle to break a hundred there. Machrihanish was fun yet challenging, a combination that is surprisingly rare. I am not suggesting the course is suitable for modern world-class championship golf: it's far too short for today's touring professional or touring amateur. Moreover, the blind shots would send world-class players into revolt. But for me (and probably for the majority of the golfing populace), Machrihanish was a golf course out of a dream.

In Machrihanish, I played my best golf in thirteen years—82, 84, 84, 81, nothing over 85 in my first ten rounds there (although nothing under 80, either). My whole game came together, putting included. My ears were sensitized to the good sounds of the game—Stark's counsel had sunk in. My mind was free of worry, and so was my swing. I didn't stand on the tee with a driver in hand and think, "I wonder where this one'll go." I wasn't worried about distance. I wasn't worried about the Phillies. I wasn't worried about Teravainen. I wasn't worried about where we would go next. We were there.

We made friends. Machrihanish was devoid of social pretension—it was an "artisans' club," in the vernacular of the country—and the members were warm and inviting. After a few days there, I was given a club tie—slim, maroon, and patterned with oystercatchers, the unofficial bird of the M. G. C. Christine and I had dinner in the clubhouse every night, and lunch often, too. Four pounds for a turkey curry dish with salad; three pounds, fifty pence for fresh snapper with green vegetables and a baked potato. Karen and Andy McNee, the couple who lived upstairs and ran the clubhouse, tended the bar, understood the television controls, cooked the food, and served it. They also made certain I had access to the club's archives. I learned that after the original ten-hole course opened for play in March of 1876, an early Machrihanish golfer wrote in his diary, "Farmer seems agreeable to our playing."

Machrihanish, I also learned, had an amazing pedigree. A local minister, the Reverend George W. Strang, who designed six of the original ten holes, was the ceremonial sod-cutter at the 1876 opening (which makes me think there must be an underlying benefit in having a holy man on hand at a golf-course baptism). Later in 1876, a man named Charlie Hunter of Prestwick reworked the course and added two holes. (Two years later Hunter designed the first five holes at Royal Troon.) In 1879, Old Tom Morris was brought in from St. Andrews for a consultation, and he came up with a plan to expand the course to eighteen holes. The course was revamped by J. H. Taylor in 1914, a year after he won his fifth and last Open. Several holes were lost to the R. A. F. during World War II, and after the war, Sir Guy Campbell, a golfing renaissance man (a player, archivist, writer, and course designer), gave the course its present configuration.

Until recently, when the club bought the land under the

course from a local farmer, there were sheep and cattle grazing on the links, with little electric fences to keep the animals off the greens. The sheep built bunkers and slept in them. In many ways, Machrihanish was a club much more nineteenth century than twentieth. Even the swings I saw there were not particularly modern. The local action was wristy and handsy, and it incorporated a big hip turn; it defied fashionable preaching. The Machrihanish golfer swung from another era.

That's because from 1920 through 1989 Machrihanish had in succession three professionals from the same family, who all taught, basically, the same method. The first of the professionals was Archibald Thomson, followed by his brother, Hector, followed by Hector's son, Arthur. All three were accomplished players and enthusiastic teachers—Archie's business stationery said, "Golf tuition 9 A.M. to 7 P.M." The legacy of the Thomson family is that the Machrihanish membership includes a lot of players making good scores with old-style swings. On a sheet listing the handicap of each of the club's three hundred and eighty-two members, I counted eighty-two players with handicaps of nine or better, including five named McMillan. I was told that at least one-third of the regulars had single-digit handicaps. That's rare.

But the consuming interest at Machrihanish (and wherever Scots congregate to play golf) was not what one individual golfer did against the course on a particular day, but what happened when one golfer played another or when two golfers joined up to play two others. I experienced this one day when Peter Kelly invited me to join him in a match against two natives. There was good conversation throughout the round, but none of it involved the match: on the first tee, the stakes were never discussed; not once did anybody ask what somebody made on a particular hole; nobody kept track of the results on a scorecard; there were no pronouncements on how the match stood. Nobody ever said anything like, "C'mon, pard, we *need* this putt!" I sensed the match was reasonably even, but I didn't really know, and didn't ask, out of respect for the local custom. Then, after all the putts were holed on the sixteenth green, our two opponents approached Kelly and me with their hands outstretched and said, "Thanks for the game." The match was over and we had lost. It was the first I knew about it.

In the clubhouse I learned that we had lost nothing, materially, just the match, and that was enough. Three people, whom I did not know, asked me about the outcome. They weren't making polite conversation with a visitor; they genuinely wanted to know. One man said, "We saw with the binoculars that you had the honor on seventeen, and it was my guess that you were all even at that point."

"Nope," I said, "closed out on the sixteenth."

"Aye, shut down on Rorke's Drift, were you," the man said, referring to the hole by its given name. "She's been the death knell of many a match."

The sixth day of our stay coincided with the Old Folks' Open, an annual tournament sponsored by Rotary International as a fund-raiser for local services for the elderly. I signed up for the event and played with two members, Karen Sutherland, a four-handicapper who had the uncanny ability to hit one straight shot after another, and Alistar Moffat, a stocky nine-handicapper who drove the ball nearly as far as Teravainen. My handicap was twelve. (The Old Folks' Open was a handicap tournament, meaning the winner of the main prize would be the person who shot the lowest score after subtracting his handicap. A handicap tournament doesn't identify the best-playing golfer, the way a professional tournament does. The handicaps theoretically even out all the players and make the day a contest to see who plays their best as measured against their norm.)

I spent the night before the Old Folks' Open twisted in the sheets, for the tournament represented the chance to show my new golf game publicly. Auchnafree had been private. At the Old Folks' Open, my score and my game would be on display, and that fact kept me up.

Morning finally arrived. As I stood on the first tee, Battery didn't look so fascinating anymore. With the long carry over the beach to the fairway, it looked positively dangerous. I was relieved when I escaped the first tee without incurring any damage, but I noticed that my line-drive tee shot rolled only about three yards after landing. The fairways and greens were soft from the previous night's rain, and the course was playing long. Moreover, we were playing in a storm wind, which came out of the northeast; I had been playing the course in the fair-weather wind, a southwesterly, for five straight days. The course felt unfamiliar and strange.

For the first time since my putting lesson from Stark, my putting was nightmarish. I was too nervous to putt well. I three-putted the first three greens and three-putted two more before the front nine was over, and went out in 45. I tried my best to use my Stark putting thought, but I couldn't concentrate on my hearing. I couldn't bring the lovely sounds of good golf to mind, because I couldn't get enough air into my lungs to get my body to function normally. All my available powers of concentration went into conversation: I was trying to maintain the charade of sanity, trying to shield Karen and Alistar from the truth, that they had drawn a lunatic for a partner, the only person in the world who could regard the Old Folks' Open as a critical test of his golfing skill. I wanted to play well so much, too much, and I could feel that fact affect my breathing. I was unable to do the things I wanted to do, things I knew how to do.

Then on the tenth hole, the par-five, I lost a ball and made a triple-bogey eight, and that calmed me. What more was there to worry about? I wasn't going to win the thing; I wasn't going to set any personal records, at least not positive ones. I played the final eight holes in five over par—nothing spectacular, but in line with my new norm—to shoot 88 for the day, 76 after subtracting my handicap. I had missed seven putts of less than four feet, and my ball-striking was not very precise, either.

Darkness always lurks in golf, and I was fighting the darkness. Even though I was playing with two of the nicest people I had met in our travels, even though the outcome of my round suggested improvement (for I had played my worst, and had still broken ninety), I cannot say I enjoyed the round. I have never thought simple enjoyment was one of the underlying virtues of the game. Golf is a damned struggle, and sometimes the struggle is defeating and sometimes it's depressing and sometimes it's encouraging and occasionally it's exhilarating. That 88 was encouraging. That's all it was, but that's a lot. I did not experience the feelings of rage that would once, not long ago, have accompanied a debacle of a round, and I knew that meant that at least in some sense I *had* improved.

Later that evening there was a marvelous dinner in the clubhouse for the participants in the Old Folks' Open. The club's captain, Malcolm McMillan, announced the winners in nearly a dozen categories. His wife, Shirley, handed out the prizes—golf shirts, gloves, balls, umbrellas. Each triumphant golfer, cheeks glowing and eyes twinkling, stood with mock bashfulness when his name was called and walked to the front of the room amid wild cheering from select friends and other inebriates, and sustained applause from everybody else. When Karen Sutherland won for Lowest Gross Score, Ladies, her table, where she sat with her lively parents and Christine and me, shook. It was a great night for clapping. The head greenkeeper, Duncan Watson, was applauded for the superb condition of the course. When a check for £710 was presented to a representative of the Rotary International, there was even more applause.

Finally, the captain announced the winner of the grand prize—the Old Folks' Open Trophy. The champion turned out to be a man named John Kiker, a urologist from New Mexico traveling with three other American physicians (a brain surgeon, a psychiatrist, and an ophthalmologist). I was surprised to learn that other Americans had been playing. I certainly hadn't seen any Americans during the preceding six days. Kiker et al. were on an annual golf trip through Scotland, and on their first journey to Machrihanish. The urologist, an eleven-handicapper, shot a gross 75, a net 64 with his handicap, and there was nobody close to that. When his name was announced, the applause was tentative; nobody in the room, except for his three friends, knew he existed. But Kiker quickly made his presence felt. In accepting the trophy, he said these words:

"When I started this trip from New Mexico in the United States ten days ago, I was hoping to play one good round, and I did. I was very lucky to have played my best round on the best course I have played in Scotland. But I am not the only beneficiary of this day. The real beneficiaries of this tournament are the people of Mackra, Mockra—the people of your community. [Appreciative laughter.] I thank you very much for having me. This is the highlight of my golf career."

As he returned to his seat, there was enthusiastic and energetic applause for Dr. John Kiker. I think everybody in the warm room felt his euphoria, and shared in it.

A couple of days later I met Mark Brenneman, a scratch-playing San Francisco art dealer who had come to Machrihanish because he liked the way the name sounded. (He had been away on a trip to St. Andrews in the first half of my Machrihanish stay.) Brenneman was a trim, youthful, and good-looking man in his middle thirties, with a blond beard and thick blond hair. Prior to coming to Machrihanish, Mark had been living on his boat in Sausalito Harbor, working as an art dealer, and wondering about the outer limits of his game. He seldom played in San Francisco, because the private clubs were expensive and difficult to join and the public courses were maddeningly overcrowded. One day he decided to leave his job, rent out his boat, and come to Scotland—a man after my own heart. He fell in love with Machrihanish. He had been there for two months and planned to stay another two. He was living in an apartment in the old defunct resort hotel, the Ugadale Arms, across the street from the first tee. He received his mail in care of the club. He was leading a sort of monkish existence, centered on playing golf and reading books.

On my final day in Machrihanish, I had an early game with Mark. It was a cool morning with a fresh breeze and a pale sky. He played a wonderful game, and was only a couple over par for the day. There was an internal serenity to him and his swing, and I found his inner calm contagious. I shot a 41 going out and had a 37, two over par, coming in: one double bogey, one bogey, six pars, and a birdie. Seventy-eight on the day. 78! It was the first time I had broken 80 since that vaporous summer, between high school and college. Right then and there, on the eighteenth green of Machrihanish, my golfing Nirvana, I declared my thirteen-year slump over. The round of 78 strokes was not an out-of-body experience. It was just (for me) good golf, something I felt I could do again. There was no question in my mind: I had improved. I felt exhilarated.

Before we left Machrihanish, I asked Mark to tell me his best swing thought. "When I'm playing well," he said, "I can see the ball on the green, before I even play my shot. It's like a movie playing backwards in my mind. The ball is already at its destination. All I have to do is make the swing. There's not a question in my mind. The only thing I see is the result."

I knew what he meant.

CHAPTER EIGHTEEN

Home

AUCHNAFREE, Machrihanish, and, finally, Dornoch, the golfing hamlet in Scotland's far northeast—that was our last stop. Dornoch, and then home. Not that we had a home, but back to the United States, anyway. We went to Dornoch in mid-September, timing our visit to coincide with Dornoch Golf Week, when Stark would be there, teaching. Stark often received offers to participate in similar instruction programs, but more often than not he declined. Standing on his legs for hours, giving group lessons, was a strain for him. Moreover, he preferred to select his own pupils and to teach each student individually, for Stark had found that every patient required his own treatment. But each year he made the trip north to Dornoch for Golf Week, out of sheer love for the place.

I signed up. I didn't want more tuition. I wanted to play the course that Stark ranked with Auchnafree and Machrihanish, and I wanted to spend more time with my mentor.

The Scots have marveled over the quality of the golf in Dornoch for generations; the Dornoch linksland—craggy and steep in places, gentle and rolling elsewhere—has been used for golf since 1616, and word of its excellence was well-spread through the Scottish Highlands long before 1906, the year the Dornoch

Golf Club was bestowed with the title "Royal." But among golfers-at-large, including well-traveled golfers in the United States, Australia, and Japan, Dornoch was until relatively recently an unknown, as obscure as Machrihanish is today. That started to change in the late 1950s, when a few prominent American golfers from Pinehurst, North Carolina, started to make the long trip up. They knew how Donald Ross—the Dornoch-born designer of the fabled No. 2 course at the Pinehurst Country Club—was shaped by his native course, and they wanted to see it for themselves. In 1964, *The New Yorker* published a piece called "North to the Links of Dornoch," a luminous story by Herbert Warren Wind extolling the virtues of Dornoch. Business has been picking up ever since. By the early 1980s, Tom Watson and Ben Crenshaw were lauding Dornoch and in 1985 the British Amateur was played there. In 1987, *Sports Illustrated* ran a long feature about Dornoch's unique charms. By 1991, with improved roads and a new bridge, Dornoch was only six hours away from St. Andrews by car. Its increased accessibility, coupled with its increased fame, gave Dornoch an automatic place on the itinerary of every serious golfer.

Going to Dornoch was not like going to Machrihanish. I went to Machrihanish without expectations. Dornoch came with a reputation. I went there fearing that it would be over-developed, over-exposed, over-golfed.

The place was wonderful. The village itself was captivating, charming, and tiny. During the day, there was just a hint of bustle. At night nothing stirred at all, except a few loose leaves on the wide lawns of the town's thirteenth-century cathedral, swirling in the dry cool winds of early autumn. The links of the Royal Dornoch Golf Club were a short walk up a hill from the center of town. More than even the Old Course, Dornoch was a parade of interesting, natural holes, one after another. On each tee I found myself saying, "Well, what have we here?" Everything was subtle, fair, and interesting.

In Dornoch, I met an American who asked me to compare Dornoch and Machrihanish. I asked him if he knew The National Golf Links of America and Shinnecock Hills, two abutting golf courses in Southampton, New York. He did, and that made things much easier.

Machrihanish, with its heaving greens and unpredictable turns, reminded me of The National Golf Links, which is often regarded as the first truly great eighteen-hole golf course in the United States. Dornoch reminded me of Shinnecock Hills, regarded by many professionals as the best of the two dozen or so U. S. Open venues used since World War II. There's something scholarly and stern about Shinnecock Hills. It is a tremendous test. The National is just fun. It has never hosted a U. S. Open and I don't think it ever could—it's too short and quirky. But as soon as you get off the eighteenth there you say, "Let's play more."

I first caddied at and played The National as a teenager (sneaking on, more often than not), and it was there that I became consciously aware of Scottish golf; The National had been described to me as the closest thing we had in the United States to a Scottish links. The course's creator, an autocratic and well-to-do native Chicagoan named Charles Blair Macdonald, became infatuated with golf as a student at St. Andrews University in the 1870s. Shortly after the turn of the century, he set out to build an American monument to golf, the first course in the United States that would rival the great courses of England and Scotland. His first mission was to find land that approximated Scottish linksland. After an exhaustive search he decided upon a tract on the shores of the Peconic Bay, three miles from the village of Southampton, on the East End of Long Island. He then built his course, over two years, incorporating design philosophies he developed on his many trips through Britain. Two of the holes at The National are reminiscent of two holes on the Old Course in St. Andrews, the Eden and the Road Hole; one imitates a hole at Prestwick called the Alps; and a fourth copies a famous hole, the par-three Redan on the west course in North Berwick. The entire layout has a Scots burr to it. The National is my favorite course in the United States, but I would not consider it a true and natural linksland course. Macdonald moved countless tons of earth to create the terrain that would accommodate the holes he envisioned. Stark told me once that true linksland is indigenous to Scotland, and I believe him.

I know of one course in the United States that is close to being a true links course, and that is Sankaty Head, on the island of Nantucket, off the southeast coast of Massachusetts. Sankaty Head is not immediately on the sea, but it is duney and sandy-soiled, windswept, treeless, and natural—a wonderful course. By no coincidence, it was designed by Donald Ross, Dornoch's most famous native son, who, as an architect, endeavored to create a linksland element in every course he built, whether he was working among North Carolina pines or California redwoods, in the clay-rich soil of Ohio or the rocky earth of New Hampshire. He never forgot the game's ancient link to sand, so evident at Dornoch (and Machrihanish, Cruden Bay, North Berwick, St. Andrews, et al.).

If you have played a lot of golf in the United States, you have no doubt played a Ross course, for he built, reworked, or routed more than five hundred of them. Few are ordinary and many are extraordinary. Three regular U. S. Open venues—Oakland Hills, outside Detroit; Oak Hill, outside Rochester; and Inverness, in Toledo—all bear the hand of Ross. My favorite Rosses include the No. 2 course in Pinehurst; The Sagamore, in Bolton Landing, New York; Torresdale-Frankford, in Philadelphia; and Sankaty Head. One trip around Dornoch and you can see immediately how Ross—who was born there in 1872 and who died in Pinehurst in 1948, a half-century after he emigrated to the United States—must have been influenced by his first golfing home. Dornoch and virtually every Ross course I have ever played share certain features: a large number of greens built on the crowns of hills; obstacle-free entrances to greens, typically, so that you can run your ball on; formidable, but never day-ruining, greenside bunkers and relatively shallow fairway bunkers; greens that are deceptively undulating; elevated tees on doglegged holes; and long, demanding par-four finishing holes.

The more time I spend in golf, the more I realize how interconnected everything within its world is. Ross became interested in course design as a teenage boy, when Old Tom Morris came up to Dornoch in 1886 to work on the course. Robert Trent Jones was similarly inspired in 1925, when Donald Ross was building Oak Hill, near Jones's boyhood home in upstate New York. Charles Blair Macdonald made his reconnaissance trips through St. Andrews in the 1890s, when Ross was studying club-making under Robert Forgan and course design under Morris. R. Forgan was the name stamped on the back of the hickory-shafted mashie that Stark had me use in my first lesson with him at Crieff. The Crieff course was designed by Willie Park, Jr., who was a mentor to Charles Blair Macdonald and the son of Old Tom Morris's chief rival. Teravainen became interested in Macdonald when he was at Yale, because the Yale course was built by Macdonald. Our mutual interest in Macdonald gave Peter and me an early affinity. Macdonald's right-hand man, Seth Raynor, built the course I grew up playing, in Bellport, Long Island. I did not know that Bellport was designed by Raynor until well into my adulthood. But I am sure that my boyhood love for the course, which has several classically Scottish holes, subconsciously rooted my interest in links golf, Scotland, and Macdonald. The world of golf—although inhabited by millions of people playing thousands of courses in dozens of countries—is, in truth, a small village.

In Dornoch I met a doctor named John Grant, who grew up in the same St. Gilbert Street house that Donald Ross did; Grant's father, Robert, had succeeded Ross as the Dornoch greenkeeper. That is the way of the small town, and that is the way of golf; the connections are everywhere. Dr. Grant, a former captain of the Royal Dornoch Golf Club, did not possess the high opinion of Ross that Ross enjoys in most corners of the globe, but he quickly acknowledged that his perspective on the architect was shaped by his father, who felt that Ross took more from Dornoch than he gave to it. This sentiment did not surprise me, either, for the citizens of a small town often retain an ambivalence toward a native who leaves and discovers success on a global scale. In Dornoch, Ross was apprenticing to become a carpenter. But carpentry led to an interest in club-making and club-making led to an interest in course design and five hundred courses later the name of Donald Ross is far more famous in America than in his native country.

Dr. Grant, the greenkeeper's son, had his lawn tended by a man named Sandy "Pipey" Matheson, who inherited his nickname from his father, a famous Dornoch bagpiper. Sandy was the last great golf character I met on my travels, a wee man, Stark's age but half his size, with fingers browned by decades of nicotine and a face reddened by decades of whisky and wind. For eyes, all Sandy had were little slits, yet he saw everything. Sandy was a caddie at Dornoch, Stark's favorite caddie in the world. "When you look at Pipey, you are looking at the face of golf," Stark had told me. Stark had called Sandy a "professional amateur" (the term I had ambitiously sought when I started my exploration). But he feared that Sandy had been changed by Dornoch's fame and the financial opportunity it represented. "It wasn't that long ago," Stark had said, "that Pipey would put a three-wood in my hand and say, 'Take the spoon and hit your little cut off the heel.' He knew your game better than you did, because he felt golf so deeply. But the last time he caddied for me, he kept giving me yardages. I said, 'Damnit, Pipey, I can get yardages from a book—put the club in my hand.' He was giving me what you Americans want from him. If Pipey gets corrupted, it's the end of golf."

Sandy was also a member at Dornoch. One day he and I played two American expatriate businessmen who lived in Paris and who were also members of Dornoch. Curtis Behrent was a tall and slender native Texan who addressed the ball with his toes pointed inward and who swung in four distinct, seemingly unconnected movements. Gary Draper, a gigantic man and a native Utahan, talked to himself, out loud, throughout his swing: "*Steady does it, Draper, elbow in, gather yourself at the top . . .*" Sandy has spent his life around golf, but he had never seen two swings, linked by partnership, quite like those two. He stared at the swings, his cigarette stuck to his lips, holding his head at a forty-five-degree angle, amazed and amused.

Sandy saw golf's endless possibilities, and that is why his fascination for it was enduring. Even when caddying for a player on a pace to shoot one hundred and ten, Sandy remained eager to find out what would happen next: "What's he going to do with *this* one?" A ten-handicapper who had once been down to a three, Sandy had a modified version of what the old Dornochians call the Dornoch Swing: he positioned the ball even with his left toe; his grip was strong; his stance was narrow; and his swing plane was flat. The result was a low-flying, long-running draw.

The four of us were playing well in a close match when we came to the thirteenth hole. It was a par-three, which measured, on this day (Sandy had told us), one hundred and thirty-seven yards, into the sharp teeth of a strong wind. Gary played first with a 7-iron. He popped his ball up and it fell thirty yards short of the green, knocked down by the wind. Curtis followed with a well-struck 6-iron, but it did not come close to the green, either. The wind was fierce.

Sandy pulled the 4-iron out of my bag and handed it to me. He pointed his nose straight into the wind and made a vertical karate chop with his right hand to show its exact direction. "Just a wee punch here, Michael," Sandy said. "Just like the lovely one you played for your third on nine." He saw all shots and he remembered all shots.

I took the 4-iron from Sandy and tried his "punch": a firm, two-thirds swing with the ball positioned toward the back of a narrowed stance, hands in front of the club face, and the toe of the club face pointed slightly in. If struck properly, the ball would climb slowly into the wind until it peaked and then fall straight down. I didn't quite pull it off. My ball hooked into a greenside bunker.

"Got your head in front of the ball just a wee bit," Sandy said. "Don't despair. A good breeze makes us all a bit jumpy."

And then Sandy got up, and took a 3-iron for this shot of only one hundred and thirty-seven yards. He played his punch shot: short and slow back, and a quick, powerful burst through the ball. His ball pierced straight into the wind without wavering. It landed twenty feet from the hole and sat right there. Gary, Curtis, and I were awed by what Sandy's know-how had produced.

"Goddamnit, Sandy, it is just such a goddamn pleasure to be here in Dornoch watching you make golf swings," Gary said.

Sandy grinned and said, "Thank you, Mr. Draper." He was not normally formal, but this was a special occasion.

On one of the last of our eight nights in Dornoch, Sandy and his wife had Christine and me for dinner in their home. I was touched by the invitation, because I'm sure that the Mathesons did not often have American visitors to their house. I knew that Sandy liked Christine, and I wanted to think that he saw me not just as a Scotsophile (as most Americans are by the time they make it up to Dornoch) but maybe even as a fellow clansman. I had already made an inquiry about the residency requirements for Scottish citizenship. We were in love with his country.

The Mathesons lived in a cozy, nineteenth-century stone house on a little street in the shadows of the cathedral. The night was cold, and upon our arrival we were shown to the living room, which was nicely warmed by a lively wood-and-coal fire. In the kitchen was a huge piece of salmon, a staple of the Highland diet. A picture of Sandy and Greg Norman rested on a hallway shelf that was jumbled with instruction books and videotapes of Open championships and Ryder Cup matches. Our dinner—poached salmon, fresh bread, boiled potatoes, steamed vegetables, and wine—was simple and good.

During tea, neighbors and relatives dropped in to watch the television. Everybody went into the living room, except Sandy and me. He got up from the table, poured himself a glass of whisky, returned to his seat. And then—I don't know why but I'll never forget it—he said, "I like your golf game, Michael."

As we sat at his kitchen table, Sandy asked for details of my golfing adventure. I told him about caddying for Teravainen and meeting Tip Anderson at the Cross Keys Bar in St. Andrews and playing Machrihanish. Sandy, in turn, told me about his admiration for Ballesteros. He told me about his youthful decision against becoming a bagpiper, a decision he later regretted. He told me about his upcoming trip to the United States to watch the Ryder Cup at Kiawah Island, in South Carolina, a gift to Sandy from Gary and Curtis.

As he talked about Dornoch, I wondered what it was like to spend a lifetime playing a single great course. I wondered what it was like to be part of the fabric of Dornoch, to know it—the village, the club, the course—so intimately and so thoroughly, to see it day after day, until the days become seasons, the seasons years, and the years a lifetime.

"Your view of the game always changes, don't you think?" Sandy said near the end of our visit. "At first, golf for me was something to do. Later it became an obsession. I'm not fanatical anymore, but the fascination will always be there. Golf will always be the framework of my life."

That made sense to me. More than any sport I know, golf provides an all-encompassing code. The game's unwritten rules elicit socially redeeming behavior; when a match is over, you shake your opponent's hand. The game's written regulations place all players on an equal footing; everybody starts from behind the tee markers. Golf is a world unto itself.

Standing at the head of a course in the early light of a late-summer day, with the fog lifting and the sheep bleating, grass clippings sticking to the sides of your shoes and the air smelling of damp wool, the golf course is a sanctuary. You wonder: *What's in store for me today?* There's hope in your voice, of course. Without hope, there is no golf.

I felt I was leaving Dornoch, and Scotland, as an improved and reconstituted golfer. And for that, I owed a debt to John Stark, for he had shown me real golf. The last time I saw him was at the banquet dinner that marked the conclusion of the Dornoch Golf Week. He had been the after-dinner speaker. When his lips finally stopped moving and he was out of words he headed out to his station wagon, wanting to get an early start on the long drive home. I walked him to his car and had a final conversation with him. This was my chance to say thank you.

"You've improved, Michael, you've improved," Stark said. He was wearing a navy blazer and the tie of the Scottish Golf

Union. I was wearing my Machrihanish tie. "You're golfing within yourself now, and that's magical. But you've got some Scot in you now, so you can no longer expect to measure your improvement simply by numbers, aye?"

I remember how his face looked as he said that: his white hair, his gold teeth, his blue eyes, ageless and wise.

"Why does the game grip us so, Michael, what do you think it is?"

He paused. I knew that I was not expected to answer. Somebody walked by us. The crunching noise of gravel underneath leather shoes built up, and then faded away.

"Because it gives us energy, Michael, that's the single best thing about the game. The better we play, the more energy we get. From now on, ask yourself, after every round, if you have more energy than before you began. 'Tis much more important than the score, Michael, much more important than the score."

And then he was off.

I am writing this shortly before New Year's Eve. In a few hours, 1991, the year I devoted to golf, will slip off into memory and the new year will commence. In a year of famine and disease, war and political tumult, I attached myself to a game. Earlier today, reading the year-end recapitulations in the paper, I was feeling a little ashamed of that fact, but now I am not. I have in front of me a book, *Golf in the Kingdom,* that says the Scots once used the word *iron* for *sword.* That must have been in the Dark Ages, when warring clans battled on the linksland. In the dawn of the Renaissance, when golf first took hold, the sandy-soiled fields were turned over to the playing of games, and, in time, iron came to refer to a certain type of golf club, and Scotland came to be peaceable. I am not suggesting that golf is a panacea, but I'm feeling good.

Christine and I came to Philadelphia and bought a house. We weren't planning to buy a house, but that's what we did. Our seven months of travel taught us that planning is overrated but that permanency is not. The mortgage man was not impressed by my 1991 income, but I convinced him that caddying was not my usual profession.

I have been up here in a windowed room off the attic for the past three months in odd hours of the day and night, writing down this report, this account of my golfing adventure. There are distractions. There's a rug in the room and I spend a lot of time practicing my putting. Occasionally, I look at the grass-stained, scarred ball that I used for my final game around the Old Course. I reminisce; I fantasize. I am surrounded by my favorite golf books and frequently dip into them: Bernard Darwin's *Golf Courses of the British Isles; The Golf Course,* by Geoffrey S. Cornish and Ronald E. Whitten; *Down the Fairway,* by Robert T. Jones, Jr.; Herbert Warren Wind's *Golf Book;* Peter Davies' *Dictionary of Golfing Terms;* Michael Murphy's *Golf in the Kingdom,* among others, and I read them now with new appreciation. The golf magazines have started to arrive. I see here that Ballesteros won the European tour's 1991 Harry Vardon Trophy as the leader of the Order of Merit. I remember how miserable he looked as he struggled to make cuts in those early tournaments—in March, in Spain—but he never looked scared, and before the year was out he had won four times, including the World Match Play. Sandy Matheson must have enjoyed watching Ballesteros in the Ryder Cup matches in late September: in the five matches in which he was involved, he won four and halved the other. The United States won back the Cup, 14½ to 13½, proving only that the best European players and the best American players continue to be evenly matched, as they have been since 1985, when the Europeans won their first Ryder Cup since 1957. I know that many people considered the 1991 Ryder Cup to be the most exciting golf they had ever seen, but I found it unseemly. In victory, the Americans raised their arms as if they were the heavyweight champions of the world. In defeat, the Europeans wore grim and pained faces, and looked as though they had just attended a funeral. I had always thought of the Ryder Cup as an international golfing get-together, but not anymore.

I received a letter from Teravainen recently. He continued to play well after the British Open and finished third at the Swiss Open. He finished thirty-eighth on the Order of Merit for the year, winning £112,536, twice as much as in any single year before. According to the official statistics, Peter was the longest driver on the tour in 1991, averaging 278.4 yards. October was a dream. He and Veronica bought a house in Singapore. Veronica had a baby girl, Taina Siying Teravainen, and Peter won a tournament, the Singapore P. G. A. Championship, an official stop on the Australian Tour. With the victory, he had earned a place on the Sony ranking of the top two hundred players in the world for the first time. At year-end, he was ranked one hundred and eighty-first, one hundred and eighty spots behind Ian Woosnam, who was named World Player of the Year by *Golf Digest.*

Peter's letter was remarkable: six dense pages, packed with information, followed a couple of days later by a two-page addendum. It took me an hour to read the letter the first time and longer the second. It was written on the stationery of a Barcelona hotel. When Peter had stayed at a hotel with its own stationery, I cannot imagine.

"The golfing gods have been good to me this year," Peter wrote. "I don't know if my good run will be over tomorrow or last a good while longer. If it continues and I can improve some more, the next five or six years will, I hope, take me to a higher level in the game. If I don't achieve anything higher than the journeyman level, that's OK, but if I have it in me to become a top fifty player in the world, I want to give myself that chance.

"I've come to realize that money is not the most important thing to me. Yes, I'm tight with money, but all I want is to have enough to take care of Veron and Taina Siying and any hospital bills I may have when I'm old. When I finished third in the Swiss Open and first in the Singapore P. G. A., money was only a very small part of my thoughts. The important thing to me was that I had won an event on one of the four major tours of the world for the first time in my life. I know that the Singapore P. G. A. is probably one of the smallest, easiest Sony ranking tournaments to win. Still, I felt a great satisfaction because no win is easy. The most important person I beat was myself. In every tournament negative thoughts can come up. The people who win are the ones who can best overcome their negative thoughts. If you haven't won, you have a big warehouse of those thoughts. After the Swiss Open I called home and told my Dad that Seve birdied the last six holes to finish one stroke ahead of me and take solo second and that I had a putt do a three-sixty on the last. I said Seve was tough. My Dad said, 'So what? You're tough, too.' It was like a smack to my brain, to remember that I had been 'tough' at other times in my career. It had been six or seven years since I was in contention and I had built up a lot of negative thoughts. I had thought a lot about my Dad during the Singapore P. G. A. and I won it for my parents, Veron, and Taina Siying. The Chinese say a baby brings luck.

"The week after the Swiss Open I was paired with Seve at the Lancôme Trophy, in Paris. You should have seen the last round. Sixteenth hole, and I'm two shots ahead of Seve. I don't care about the tournament—I just want to beat Seve. I don't know if it's my imagination or what, but I get the feeling that Seve's actually aware that I'm ahead of him, and he doesn't want to lose. I hit a killer Whiplash that looks like it's never going to come down and my legwork has me dancing all around the tee. The caddies have been waiting all day for this moment and they're loving it. Seve is stunned. He takes a long time preparing for his drive and he tries to psych himself up by taking six or seven practice swings. He backs off the shot once, then gets back in to try to match this monster drive and crazy swing. He swings so hard all he produces is a quick snap hook into the trees. Billy Foster, his caddie, has to bite his finger to stop from laughing.

"I sometimes wonder what it would be like to be seventeen again, a senior at Tabor, racing around the Kittansett course, trying to get in as many holes as possible before we had to go back to school for dinner. If you ever have a chance to play Kittansett, especially in the spring, you'll see why I have a few wind shots in the bag. Maybe I'm seeing it with a youthful, enthusiastic, dreaming mind, but Kittansett is still my favorite course in the world. I wouldn't want to play a tournament there, though—it's too tight. I don't know if I'd ever want to play there again. I think I only want to play it in my mind, as a seventeen-year-old dreamer."

I also recently received a letter from John Stark, written in a beautiful and artistic hand. He quoted from Burns, the Bible, and Ballesteros, and included a report on the 1991 Auchnafree Open.

"For the Auchnafree Open we had a field of twenty-one players," Stark wrote. "One Archie MacDiarmid of Locherlour, a sheep farmer, won the event with a score of 65. I was confined to the barbecue by the Doctor—had a recurrence of arthritis in the spine—but it looks as though we have it checked, and I intend to get the clubs out more in the new year. I wrote a letter to Sir James Whitaker thanking him for his kindness in allowing us to play the Auchnafree and received a courteous reply assuring us we could play annually. So we will do that, playing on the course laid out by our late friend, Shepherd John Pollock, playing for the trophies that he first presented, and in his memory. I hope someday you will come and play."

As I sit here, I am thinking back to the last time I saw John Stark, leaning against his car, parked under a fragrant evergreen that stood straight into the final moments of the blue-and-black Dornoch dusk. I can hear the wind pass haltingly through its needles. Stark told me to come by his pro shop in Crieff on the drive south to Heathrow Airport in London. He said he had a present for me—the old hickory-shafted mashie with which he gave me my first lesson. I never made it to Crieff, and I'm glad I didn't. I like knowing that there's an old iron, hand-forged by a man in St. Andrews named R. Forgan, stuffed into a closet in the back of Stark's cluttered office, waiting for my return.

In the meantime, I'm eager for the arrival of spring.